The New Testament
A Guide to Its Writings

GÜNTHER BORNKAMM

The New Testament
A Guide to Its Writings

translated by Reginald H. Fuller
and Ilse Fuller

FORTRESS PRESS   Philadelphia

This book is a translation of *Bibel—Das Neue Testament. Eine Einführung in seine Schriften im Rahmen der Geschichte des Urchristentums,* copyright © 1971 by Kreuz-Verlag in Stuttgart, Germany.

Library of Congress Catalog Card Number 73–79009

ISBN 0–8006–0168–8

Second printing 1975

5421K75   Printed in U.S.A.   1-168

Table of Contents

Foreword

"For everything there is a season, and a time for every matter under heaven" (Eccles. 3:1). In every time and season the New Testament has raised questions for the people who read it. Whether we are informed adherents of the Christian tradition or know little about it, or perhaps have drifted away from it, our reading of the New Testament confronts us with questions of different sorts and of varying degrees of urgency. This book is an effort to deal with some of these questions. At the same time it is an effort to introduce the reader to new methods of biblical investigation and new possibilities of biblical interpretation. The two efforts in fact are interrelated and depend very much on one another.

Naturally, a guide such as this cannot hope to survey in an exhaustive way the contents of all the New Testament writings. Our hope is rather to convey an impression of their rich variety and diverse history and to bring out their focal ideas and central concerns in such a way as to stimulate the reader's own thoughtful study of the writings themselves. The important thing is not so much that he become acquainted with the generally accepted findings of modern biblical scholarship as that he become personally caught up in the exciting process of inquiry and discovery. The Bibliography at the back of the book may prove useful in this connection.

Since space is so limited in a little book of this sort, we will have to be highly selective in our choice of topics. The first three Gospels and the letters of Paul will therefore be treated more extensively than the other New Testament writings. We will not rehearse the problems involved in establishing for each writing the earliest and most authentic text. We will make no attempt to trace the history of New Testament interpretation. Nor will we discuss those other writings of the early church which failed to find acceptance in the biblical canon.

As regards sequence of topics, it has proven impossible to deal with the individual writings and groups of documents in the specific order in which they presently appear in the New Testament. Nor could we follow strictly the chronological order in which the various books were probably written. We have sought rather an arrangement intended simply to further our purpose of providing a clear and simple guide to the New Testament writings.

Günther Bornkamm

Introduction:
The "Charter" of
the Christian Faith

The purpose of this book is to ease the modern reader's approach to the New Testament. At times, however, where the subject itself requires, the result may be just the opposite: things will seem even more complicated and difficult than before. For many of our contemporaries the New Testament is obviously a closed book. To be sure, the Bible is still translated into more languages than any other book, and sold in greater numbers throughout the world. It is still regarded as "the book of books," in a class by itself. But unlike other current best sellers, for all the copies in print the Bible is practically unknown. Ignorance of it abounds and men are more estranged from it than ever before.

One of the reasons for this strange turn of affairs undoubtedly has to do with the Christian tradition itself, which has been deeply shaken by the changed circumstances of our modern world. Traditions of course are and always have been essential in human society; without them life would be unthinkable. And whoever would deny the need for traditions or try to do away with them is in reality destroying the foundations of his own existence; he need not wonder then why his life is buffeted about like a ship without a rudder until it finally founders on the sandy shoals. But age-old traditions, such as the Christian tradition, unfortunately have a way of occasionally stirring up a little dust. They also— and this is even worse—have a way of casting a heavy pall of dust like a dark shroud over what was once a dynamic and provocative history. Once Christianity becomes merely a matter of tradition and nothing more, it can still claim to set forth the past in a reliable way, but it is no longer capable of making that history come alive in the present—because, as mere tradition, it refuses to face up to the changed circumstances in the contemporary world. Whenever church tradition has refused to confront the present, it has tended to lock up its living history as in a sacred tabernacle or a musty cupboard, always with the honorable intention of sheltering it from the corrosive influence of the spirit of the times. But history thus cautiously sealed off from the present is reduced to silence; it no longer has anything to say.

How can the appeal of a particular history, especially that which is attested in the Bible, gain a hearing? The answer may surprise some people: it will be heard best if we leave it in its own time, place, language, and world, and do not immediately rush to appropriate it for ourselves. Anyone who cannot bear the remoteness and strangeness of the biblical figures and witnesses, and hence forces upon them prematurely the perspectives, ideas, and outlook of his own age— or instead runs away from his own age and pretends to be a contemporary of the Bible—rules out in advance any real encounter with the texts. By refusing to let them say what they have to say, he denies them the chance of entering into real dialogue with the kind of partner to whom they would address themselves today, the person who will not only listen to the texts but also put questions to them in return.

The task of biblical scholarship as it uses the tools of linguistic and historical criticism is simply to let the biblical authors have their own say. The scholar must bring out the intention of the New Testament writings. To the best of his ability he must try to understand their original meaning. Then, like a ferryman taking his cargo from one shore to the other, he must "translate" it all from biblical times and the biblical world to our own. His task is to transport or carry, not just to add more building blocks to a biblical mausoleum. How far such a "translation" will succeed can never be gauged in advance. The project is hampered not only by limitations in the scholar's ability but also by the fact that the Bible is a historical document. It would be an illusion to suppose that everything that stands between its covers still speaks today with undiminished validity.

Rightly understood, the time-bound and historically conditioned character of the Old and New Testaments is not something to be deplored, as if it made the Bible merely a pitiful relic of the past. It is rather a clear indication that the biblical witnesses and writers always addressed their message to specific persons in particular situations. The varied character and diverse origins of the writings are therefore never to be denied. The common human tendency to neglect or ignore the historical uniqueness of the particular occasion has left its traces everywhere, even within the New Testament itself—a clear indication that the problem of achieving a correct and currently vital understanding is one that has been inherent in Christianity from the very beginning. Indeed, this is why Christian spokesmen, unlike the devotees of many other religions, have never been able to content themselves with merely celebrating holy rites and repeating sacred formulas.

Here at the outset we may mention just a few points where common opinion may need correction. False assumptions about the New Testament can make the understanding of it more difficult.

1. There is, for example, the fallacious notion that the New Testament was always the "Holy Scripture" of Christianity. The fact is that from the beginning scriptural status was accorded exclusively to the Old Testament. The New Testament did not even exist when Christianity began. The formulation of the New Testament canon with its twenty-seven writings, all of them very different from one another, was a gradual development that occurred between the end of the second century and the fourth century. It should be noted that this "canon" (a term derived from the Greek word for standard or norm) is the result not of a collecting process, but of a sifting process, a selection which involved the setting apart of certain writings considered to be normative from a mass of other ecclesiastical and heretical literature. Some of this other literature we still possess intact, some of it has survived only in fragments, and much of it has of course been lost altogether. So far as we can judge from the extant evidence, some of the principles on which the selection was made—such as direct, or perhaps only mediated, apostolic authorship—have turned out to be erroneous. Yet in the final result the selection itself was a happy one. There is hardly a single extracanonical writing we know of that we would

wish had been included in the New Testament canon. The most we can say is that there may be some doubt as to whether all of the writings presently included are equally deserving of inclusion. In any case, the New Testament canon is a product of an earthly, human history. It did not drop down as a revelation from heaven. The impulse behind its formation, by the way, came not from within the mainstream of the church but from Marcion, who in the middle of the second century founded a counterchurch. With a rigid dogmatism based on a crude misinterpretation of Paul, Marcion rejected the Old Testament. He regarded it as the revelation not of the Christian God of love but of another God, an inexorably "righteous" Jewish God. Marcion made his rigorous selection of available Christian scriptures accordingly. The battle against this Marcionite heresy, with its dualism and denial of creation, played an important part in the formation of the church's canon.

2. The concept of a "New Testament" as applied to the canonical corpus of Christian scriptures came only gradually to be accepted. It was originally intended not as the title of a book but as a theological affirmation, signifying both the unity and the difference between the revelation of God in the Old Covenant and its fulfillment in Christ. The concept has its roots in 2 Cor. 3:6 ff., where Paul takes up the Old Testament promise of a new covenant in Jer. 31:31 and places the "old" and the "new" covenants (law and gospel) side by side, at the same time coordinating them with one another. Already in the Septuagint (the Greek translation of the Old Testament), the Hebrew word for "covenant" in Jer. 38:31 was translated *diathēkē,* which originally meant ordinance, dispensation, economy of salvation. In Latin the

Greek word in turn was rendered *testamentum*. This Latin term of course did not mean the last will and testament of a dying person but carried with it the force of the Greek meaning. In this roundabout way "Old Testament" and "New Testament" became the designations of the two parts of the biblical canon.

3. Compared to the Old Testament, the theme of the New Testament appears amazingly simplified. It may be reduced to a single name, Jesus Christ. This thematic difference corresponds to the difference between the history documented in the two Testaments. In the Old Testament we have a tumultuous sequence of events covering a thousand years of history, from Israel's exodus out of Egypt through its many ups and downs to its loss of independent statehood and the reconstitution of the Jewish nation after the exile. In the course of all that history we meet a mass of events, facts, and dates, and the documentation which supports them. Contrasted with this far-reaching, vivid, and rich history, the New Testament appears meager in the extreme, even if the national limitations of the Old Testament have been transcended to a radical degree. Only from the New Testament perspective can we speak meaningfully of a turning point in history. But this turning point is obviously grounded in a radical concentration upon Jesus Christ. Jesus and his history overshadow everything else. All the other personalities which cross the pages of the New Testament—his disciples and opponents, believers and unbelievers, the possessed and the healed, Pilate and the Romans—are important only insofar as they appear in the light, or shadow, of Jesus. The early Christians were not really concerned with the bare sequence of historical facts at all, nor with describing the earthly work

and fate of Jesus himself. Their concern with Jesus and his history was really a concern with an event of ultimate and saving significance that was transpiring therein between God and the world.

4. Like the books of the Old Testament, the New Testament writings as they are found in our Bibles fall into three groups: historical books (the Gospels and Acts), books of instruction (the Letters), and one prophetic book (Revelation). This arrangement and designation is actually open to question, because it involuntarily carries with it the false impression that the first group contains the past history which is the basis of faith, the second a system of Christian doctrine valid for all time, and the third a picture of the future and of the end of the world. But closer study will show that this oversimplified division of time into three periods is untenable. For all of the New Testament writings refer back in faith to the Christ event, just as they all, though in different ways, are concerned with the present and the future. This will become evident as we proceed.

5. Finally, we should be careful of the conventional dogmatic view, nourished by the formation of the canon and by church tradition, that the New Testament is a summary of binding Christian doctrine or a kind of doctrinal norm. Anyone who shares this illusion is bound to ignore the significant differences that exist in the New Testament—between the four Gospels (especially between the so-called synoptics and John), Acts and Paul, Paul and James, and so on—and to harmonize the texts so as to make all the New Testament authors say pretty much the same thing. While it is certainly right to look for a common theme in the New Testament, it is quite wrong to minimize the differences and contradictions.

Cutting and twisting things in Procrustean fashion is the worst of all possible procedures for interpreting the New Testament.

After all these words of caution we can now give a direct and positive answer to the question, What is the New Testament? It is the "charter"* of Christian faith, but not in the sense in which either the historian or the lawyer normally understands that term. The New Testament is a "historic" document all right, not in an archival sense, however, but only in the sense of its being the primal proclamation, the original and foundational appeal to faith. It also possesses a "binding" character, not in the sense of imposing a legal obligation to some uniform system of doctrine, however, but only in the sense that it sets forth the many varied expressions and effects of early Christian faith in such a way as to involve the reader in the ongoing struggle between faith and knowledge, the personal battle between truth and error.

* [*Ur-kunde.* Unhyphenated, the word normally means "document," "primary evidence." The author here hyphenates the compound deliberately in order to bring out the distinct connotations of its separate parts: "original" and "proclamation."—Trans.]

1. Jesus and the Gospel

Whoever would speak appropriately about the New Testament cannot rest content with merely summarizing its contents, enumerating its books, and giving an account of their origins, authors, addressees, and the occasions for which they were written. He must speak of Jesus, of him who is not only encountered everywhere within this "book" but also in every sense of the word comes before it. This priority of Jesus is a temporal and historical priority: Jesus is not the author of the New Testament, nor of any of its books; he never left us a single written sentence, nor was he technically a scriptural exegete like the scribes—and these well-known facts are worth remembering. His priority, however, is also one of substance: every statement in the New Testament must be understood and evaluated with reference to him as its criterion.

Obviously, this is easier said than done. It is no secret that our historical knowledge of Jesus is sketchy in the extreme. The only sources of historical information about him are contained in our Gospels. Other scattered references, e.g., in later Jewish writings or in Roman histories, are relatively superficial and worthless notices at second or third hand. Further, what can be gleaned from apocryphal (i.e., extra-canonical) Christian writings consists almost entirely of later outgrowths and products of fantasy. It is hardly likely that another "authentic" gospel will turn up some day in Palestine, Egypt, or anywhere else. Yet our four canonical Gospels contain no shorthand notes of Jesus' sermons, no official records about his deeds and fate, no biography in either the ancient or the modern sense of the term.

And yet it would be senseless and quite unjustified to leave a blank space at this critical juncture or to insert a mysterious X. For the gospel tradition has unmistakably preserved—though to what extent may be disputed—the word of the historical Jesus himself, and generally in such a way that each fragment reflects the whole. That is why we do not need in every case to establish by critical methods the authenticity of a particular saying, or to reconstruct his preaching as a whole from the nucleus we have.

THE MESSAGE OF JESUS

It is not our task here to give a complete presentation of Jesus. We will confine ourselves to the center of his proclamation, his message about the coming of the kingdom of God. It is summarized for us, albeit in the language of the early Christian mission, in the Gospel of Mark: "The time has come; the kingdom of God is upon you; repent and believe the gospel" (1:15).

Among those who first heard Jesus such words as God's kingdom, kingly rule or reign, were certainly not unknown. But these terms had been strangely neglected by Pharisaic piety, relegated to the background, and were no longer alive with assurance and eager expectation. Religious circles had, as it were, dragged these words along with them into their ghetto and into the jargon of their guild. For example, people spoke of "taking the yoke of the kingdom of God upon oneself"; by this they meant clinging in the face of heathen polytheism to faith in the one God, and obeying the letter of the law in the hope that at the last day the kingdom of God would once again become manifest. But their real, living expectation was centered upon the national Messiah, who at the end time would break the yoke of foreign rule and restore to the Jewish people an independent state. On a universal scale, Jewish expectancy with regard to the end confronts us in the grandiose designs of apocalyptic, with its fantastic pictures of the decline and fall of this old and wicked world, of judgment and the age of paradise it is to usher in. In orthodox piety God's rule and kingdom is reduced to a private matter, and in apocalyptic it is replaced by a broad and complicated theological picture which blackens the world and makes it demonic so as to throw into greater relief the glory of the transcendent world to come. Thus the reign of God was in one way or the other pushed to the side, relegated to a transcendent sphere. It had become an empty cipher.

Another variant is offered by the political and theocratic revolutionary movement whose members were known as "Zealots," or fanatic nationalists. They took the rule of God in bloody earnest, stirring up revolt and using all the methods of guerrilla warfare to force the coming of God's kingly rule and to eliminate collaborators and lawbreakers. This movement culminated in the Jewish-Roman war and led to the destruction of Jerusalem.

If we keep the contemporary background in view it becomes clear that Jesus took up a controversial word, laden with all sorts of political and religious freight, and made it the content of his message. It was far from being a discarded, forgotten term, dragged up from oblivion. But how did this happen? For both sides Jesus was an alien and scandalous figure, an intolerable provocation, an insult to the sheltered coteries of piety. He refused to underwrite their religious activities, and broke through the barriers they had so jealously erected between the righteous and the unrighteous. Nor did he share the wild fantasies of the apocalyptic visionaries (Luke 12:56). Yet he was equally useless to the Zealots. He would not echo their trumpet call to battle and revolt (Mark 12:13 ff.), even though in our day it has once more become fashionable to regard Jesus as one of their party.

It is difficult to find a formula to describe the rule of God, whose imminent advent Jesus announced in his message. This is not because it is a mystical reality but because it is an event, a happening, in which God's future and the present life of men—whom Jesus confronts with his word, his work, and his conduct—encounter one another and open to one another. The rule of God is both God's coming to save the world and the present earthly life of man as viewed in the light of the liberating nearness of God.

Jesus' message about the kingdom of God would be unthinkable without the expectation of the future and the end which was current in Jewish apocalyptic. He shares with his contemporaries the eschatological conviction that the end of the world is imminent (Luke 17:24 ff.). Anyone who fails to see these connections is bound to make the kingdom of God in Jesus' preaching a timeless, universal idea of the supreme ethical good, as has often happened before. The historically conditioned character of Jesus' preaching has, one might say, an ambivalent meaning. Unlike the timelessness of general thought, his message is anchored to its unrepeatable temporal past and mind-set, and is at the same time inseparable from time and history.

In the last analysis, the reign of God as proclaimed by Jesus has no further need of the traditional apparatus of apocalyptic, and in any case no longer accepts it lock, stock, and barrel. Such notions as the Messiah, the dramatic end of the world, the Last Judgment, the Son of God as judge of the world, and the new life in paradise are dispensable. Wherever these themes do occur in Jesus' message they obviously function as elements in his language, but are not, as they were for his contemporaries, constitutive for his teaching. Moreover, in many instances we can prove, or at least conjecture, that they are later creations of the believing community. It is significant that Jesus nowhere personally requires people first to recognize him as an eschatological functionary, nor does he make the truth of his message stand or fall by such a recognition. This is all the more remarkable since, according to his preaching, the kingdom of God is already breaking through in his word, his activity, and his conduct. The "stronger one" who ends the rule of Satan and seizes his prey is already here (Mark 3:27; Luke 11:20; Matt. 13:16 f.).

What is absolutely decisive is God's coming in mercy. God is no longer the prisoner of his own transcendence, incarcerated in the nebulous future to which pious tradition and expectation had consigned him, leaving the world to its own devices. Rather, he comes to the world, so close, so humanly close, as in the ordinary events described in Jesus' parables (Matt. 13:24 ff., 31 f., 33 f., 44 ff.; 18:23 ff.; 20:1 ff.; Luke 16:1 ff.). Hence it is foolish to try to calculate God's future

(Luke 17:20). Whoever hears the challenge of the hour no longer has any time for such escapism. Rather, he accepts his allotted time in a qualified but no longer merely chronological sense. Hence Jesus' charge: "Be alert, be wakeful" (Mark 13:33).

The reign of God is both future and present; it is not dissolved into an unqualified present. The poor of the first beatitude in the Sermon on the Mount are not laughing at the time. The hungry are not expected to regard their starvation as satiety (Luke 6:20 ff.; Matt. 5:3 ff.). The opening petitions of the Lord's Prayer (Luke 11; Matt. 6) assume a desperate need. God's name is being blasphemed and his kingdom has not yet come. But neither does Jesus promise another, better world, for the God who comes is already at work on the stage.

The nearness of God confronts a man with his neighbor, whether friend or foe, and asserts that neighbor's claim upon him. It is from this angle that Jesus' sovereign attitude toward the law must be understood, also his proclamation of the will of God—spoken with authority and not as the scribes (Matt. 7:28 f.)—and indeed his own conduct, which was blasphemous in the eyes of his opponents and provoked the fatal conflict with the authorities of his people. As he draws near, God shatters even the murderous structures of society in which everything and everybody is hopelessly enmeshed: the pious and impious, the privileged and the outcast, Jews and Gentiles. The supposedly solid structures of the existing world, with its unassailable norms and religious sanctions, are called into question by Jesus' command of love.

Jesus proclaims the hour of the approaching reign of God. This is what gives unity to his message of salvation and his call to repentance. "Happy are the eyes that see what you are seeing! I tell you, many prophets and kings wished to see what you now see, yet never saw it; to hear what you hear, yet they never heard it" (Luke 10:23–24). "Repent; for the kingdom of heaven is upon you" (Matt. 4:17). Note that he does not say, "You will go to heaven by and by, when your time on earth with all its miseries is done." No, he says, "God is coming to you!" Nor does his call to repentance lay down any conditions which have to be met first (if you repent, then . . .). Instead, the announcement of God's coming is made first. It is the basis of all that follows, for his reign has drawn near. Thus repentance does not mean merely withdrawing within oneself in remorse, but opening oneself to the future of God. It is a movement not backward, but forward.

THE GOSPEL AND THE GOSPELS

Gospel "History"

This incomplete capsule summary of the message of Jesus is drawn from the first three Gospels. Yet strictly speaking, that is not what they really are all about. Still less is it the content of the Fourth Gospel, an independent theological interpretation of Jesus' story which will receive separate consideration in due course (see below, pp. 131 ff.). But neither do the first three Gospels, the so-called synoptics, simply recount a history lived out like other histories in time and space. The limitations of time and space and the norms they set are shattered. If what the Gospels narrate is to be called a history at all—and to deny this would certainly be absurd and mistaken—it is evidently, at least by our standards, a unique kind of history, in a class all by itself. That is to say, there is no direct road from the "historical" Jesus to the story narrated in the Gospels, still less to what the later doctrine of the church since the New Testament affirms about this Jesus.

Those who have grown up in the Christian tradition as it was accepted for many centuries and who cling to it uncritically will boggle at what we have just said, and refuse to admit that there is any problem here at all. They accept the Gospels as they stand, as historically reliable. They explain the remarkable combination of natural and supranatural in the Gospels in terms of the unity of the divine and human natures in the person of Jesus. Once this confession of "faith" has been made, there is a perfectly natural solution to all riddles. The eternal Son of God, who came down from heaven and was miraculously born of a virgin, spent his life on earth proving his divinity by countless miracles. Then he rose from the dead, and finally he ascended miraculously back to heaven from whence he came. Thus Jesus' life story as narrated by the Gospels passed without break into the later teaching of the apostolic church. According to this kind of biblicism, it is too bad that skepticism has thrown doubt upon this consistent picture, and that a godless theology has succumbed to the spirit of the age, even aiding and abetting it.

But this point of view has been irreparably shattered by the rise of a quite different understanding of the world and of history. That is why historical-critical biblical scholarship was right to reject the supranaturalism derived from the world picture of antiquity and the Middle Ages, even though orthodoxy stubbornly defends it to this day. Biblical scholarship has been concerned to loosen the ties which, as Albert Schweitzer has said, "chained Jesus to the rock of ecclesiastical doctrine." In the process it has opened up a wealth of new insights, posed new questions, and pointed to new ways. No longer is it possible to return to the faith of the fathers with its traditional metaphysic.

But have the scholars really opened the way to the Jesus proclaimed in the Gospels? To this question we can only answer no. For, paradoxical though it may sound, even the era of the so-called Life of Jesus theology,* despite its ostensible rejection of orthodox biblicism, was still trapped in the same perspective. It still believed it possible to build a bridge which led directly from the "historical" Jesus to the Jesus of the Gospels. Like their predecessors, the scholars who pursued the so-called quest of the historical Jesus regarded the Gospels primarily as biographies. Of course the gospel narratives were held to have been often embroidered by later piety and colored by the occasionally primitive opinions of the narrators; in some places the narratives had been truncated, in others padded with fantasy. But essentially they were considered biographical in nature.

It would be wrong, however, to throw out the baby with the bath water. Tendencies to embellish certainly are to be found in the Gospels. And even though the critical work of scholars in that earlier generation did sometimes take a wrong turn, it produced results which can hardly be contested today. But the presuppositions which undergirded it have proven erroneous. Wrong criteria were applied to the sources, and questions were posed which the Gospels could not possibly answer. Although the gospel writers were certainly interested in Jesus' history, theirs was a quite different interest from that of biographers and historians, whether ancient or modern.

* [For many of its more important documents see The Lives of Jesus Series edited by Leander E. Keck (Philadelphia: Fortress, 1969–).— Trans.]

We will go into that further in due course. For the moment let us simply repeat that the presuppositions which used to be imposed upon the Gospels by the scholars were both naïve and erroneous. The bridges which were built with such unflagging ingenuity, between the "historical" Jesus and the tradition about him, have turned out to be illusory.

But this has not destroyed the popularity of a certain type of literature based on the crumbling foundations of the old quest. Even today such Lives of Jesus enjoy widespread publicity. They keep appearing at more or less regular intervals. Such publications always have one thing in common. In a tendentious, anti-Christian way they pretend to disabuse a public long deceived and kept in ignorance by the church and its spokesmen, whose intentions were all too obvious. At last these honest authors have come along to give the public the unadulterated truth. Now people can be told the latest scientifically proven facts, and Christianity will be unmasked at last as a hoax! Johannes Lehmann, for example, takes the Dead Sea Scrolls, which have been well known since 1947, and grotesquely misinterprets them in an effort to prove that Jesus was an Essene Jew and that his message was simply a rehash of the religious teachings of the Qumran sect—a fact which the New Testament writings and the church's teaching have consistently sought to hide.* People who write that kind of thing think they are being avant-garde. Actually, however, they are belated stragglers along a well-worn path. They pervert the assured results of scholarship, theological and otherwise. But that, for the most part, is something their readers cannot see, because it is hidden by all the camouflage.

* Johannes Lehmann, *Jesus-Report. Protokoll einer Verfälschung* [A report on Jesus: the documentation of a forgery] (1970).

The Life of Jesus approach failed to make the Gospels accessible. So did the orthodox-biblicist approach and the long gallery of Jesus portraits which resulted in the old quest. This is generally realized today, and scholars rightly take that fact pretty well for granted. Indeed it will be borne out below as we interpret the texts. The only way forward is to pursue our inquiry along totally different lines and abandon the outmoded Life of Jesus approach.

The Gospel

The very term "gospel" encourages us to take a different line. It is true that only one of the evangelists (Mark) uses this word as a title for his book (1:1). But the church was quite right when it applied the same title to the works of the other three evangelists as well. It was very helpful for our understanding that this was done.

However, the choice of the term "gospel" confronts us with an enigma. In the language of early Christianity the term does not refer to a particular literary form. The gospel was in existence long before the Gospels were written, but the term then meant something entirely different. The Greek word for "gospel," *euangelion,* means "good news," "glad tidings." It probably comes from the language of the earliest Hellenistic Christian mission. It was in this context that the word was first used in a clearly religious sense, with specific reference to the message of salvation accomplished in Jesus Christ. The word occurs in this sense sixty times or so in the Pauline and deutero-Pauline literature, always in the sense of a verbal proclamation which has constantly to be repeated and heard anew. In the very nature of the case there cannot be more than one gospel (Gal. 1:6). All there can be is a more precise indication of its origin ("the gospel of God") and a more precise specification of its content ("the gospel of Jesus Christ"). Paul often uses the term "gospel" standing alone; he could do this because its meaning was clear and well known.

It is hard for us nowadays to recognize the real meaning and import of the word "gospel." After centuries of Christian tradition the term has become clericalized and has worn thin, like the similar word "preaching." Originally, "gospel" meant nothing less than the announcement or proclamation, the making present and real of an epochal event—God's liberating action in the coming, death, and resurrection of Christ, which has to be grasped in faith. It was to this end that Paul, called to be a "messenger and slave" of Jesus Christ, undertook his mission to the Gentiles (Rom. 1; Gal. 1).

True, the message speaks of a particular history, not a timeless or mythical event. Paul can sum up the whole gospel in his startling phrase, "the word of the cross" (1 Cor. 1:18 ff.). However, by this he does not mean the final tragic injustice done to Jesus once upon a time in Jerusalem. Paul did not just want to awaken the sympathy or indignation of his hearers. What impression would that have made in a world where countless disobedient slaves and political rebels were executed in the same cruel manner? And how could Paul have reinforced such news by calling it a message of salvation and joy? No, Paul preaches Christ crucified, whom God made "Lord over all" (Phil. 2:6 ff.), as a divine manifesto "openly displayed" before the eyes of the whole world for its salvation (Gal. 3:1). He proclaims a new day of creation whose light shines in the gospel (2 Cor. 4:4 ff.).

But there is no indication that Paul had any particular place in his gospel for the earthly life of Jesus prior to his death and resurrection. There is no mention of what the Gospels tell, not a word about Jesus' preaching or the approach of God's kingly rule, nothing about Jesus' casting out demons, healing the sick, debating with the Pharisees and scribes, or consorting with tax collectors, sinners, and outcasts. Nor does Paul ever mention the parables of Jesus or the Lord's Prayer.

It is of course in Paul's letters that this strange and oft lamented state of affairs is most obvious. Yet in their concentration upon Christ's death, resurrection, and exaltation, and in their omission of the earthly history of Jesus, Paul's letters represent a common pattern of early Christian preaching, a pattern which continues all through the later writings composed about the same time as the Gospels or even after them.

In the earliest times this "kerygma" or preaching found its most concise expression in brief résumés of Christian doctrine (e.g., Rom. 1:3 f.; 1 Cor. 15:3 ff.; 2 Tim. 2:8), in creedal statements (1 Cor. 8:5 f.; Rom. 10:8 f.; Acts 8:37), and in hymns and songs (Phil. 2:6 ff.; Col. 1:15 ff.; 1 Tim. 3:16). All of these formulas are forerunners of the creed as we know it in the church today. Yet most of these biblical statements are free from the aftertaste of the stereotyped phrases and archaic or meaningless propositions which burdens the understanding of the Christian creeds that have come down to us. They are also free from any uniformity; no two propositions are identical. The proclamation is couched in constantly new formulations. The messianic titles change according to the speaker's level of understanding— his origin, language, and mode of thought—and that of his audience, each title expressing the faith that the salvation wrought in Jesus is both a present reality and a future hope

—Jesus as the one who is the same yesterday, today, and for ever (Heb. 13:8).

Originally even the two words "Jesus Christ" were an early Christian confession. They were not just a man's ordinary first and last names, like the name Pontius Pilate. Their conjunction must be understood in two directions: Jesus is the messianic *Christ,* the one who brings salvation; and the messianic title denotes the historical person *Jesus,* without substituting for him some mythical figure. The combination and coalescence of the two names, the earthly and human name (Jesus) and the divine title of majesty transcending the limitations of a specific human existence at a particular time and place in history (Christ), has always been an essential part of the Christian message. And it is just this that has caused so much offense and evoked so much dissent from the beginning until now.

The Gospels

The difference between the gospel as we have described it and the Gospels is obvious. The Gospels are narratives of the earthly history of Jesus, culminating in the passion and Easter stories. There is nothing of this in the gospel. The end and goal of the gospel is the beginning, foundation, and content of all proclamation and thought in the Gospels.

What, then, is the connection between the gospel and the Gospels? Did the tradition put the first four books of the canon under the wrong heading? As we shall see, neither the tradition nor even Mark in his day could have chosen a more suitable or happy term.

But what precisely is the connection? It would be tempting to argue as follows: Taken as they stand, the Gospels, at least the first three of them, have hardly anything to do with

the gospel in the sense of kerygma. They are completely independent of the post-Easter message of faith. Fortunately,
however, they have preserved, at least to some extent, the
picture of the historical Jesus. Only here and there have they
touched it up in the light of the later creed.

Alternatively it could be argued that the gospel and the
Gospels were closely associated right from the beginning,
though each had its own particular function. The Jesus tradition invariably accompanied the proclamation of salvation in
the kerygmatic sense. From the beginning it provided illustrative material for missionary preachers, preachers in the
congregations, and the authors of the New Testament writings apart from the Gospels. The intention was to make clear
just who this Jesus was for whom the kerygma made such
amazing claims. The authors of the other New Testament
writings could take it for granted that their readers and
hearers were familiar with the story of the earthly Jesus, so
there was no need for them to refer to it in so many words.

At first sight, both explanations look very attractive. But
both are misleading. There is little to support them in the
texts themselves. Of course we know very little about the
preaching of the early church. But we can be sure that these
assumptions, at least taken as they stand and without qualifi-
cation, are false.

Nevertheless, despite the differences between them, the
gospel and the Gospels have a common origin. For the Gospels and the Jesus tradition they enshrine are rooted in the
certainty of the resurrection of Christ. In all their variety
they are manifestations of this one faith. It may sound like
nonsense, but we venture to say that the gospel story begins
with its end. For Jesus' Jewish opponents and for the Roman
occupying power, there could be no doubt that his end on

the cross was the annulment of his story. For the disciples, on the other hand, the appearances of the risen One and their experience of his presence in the Spirit meant that his end was a new beginning, in the sense of a final and absolute act of God for the salvation of the world. Men had condemned Jesus, but God turned their no into a yes. In that yes God committed himself irrevocably to the world that rejected him.

In the earliest community this certainty was not just the private property of a few visionaries or the private opinion of a select few. The earliest and most reliable list of the appearances of the risen One (1 Cor. 15:1–11) culminates in the assertion of Paul, which guarantees all the others: "But what matter, I or they [i.e., the other apostles]? This is what we all proclaim, and this is what you believed." Even the opponents he is arguing with in 1 Corinthians 15 never doubted the message; their dispute was only with what Paul deduced from it. The early Christians expressed this faith in many different ways. The story of the empty tomb as we have it in the New Testament and in the apocryphal gospels, a story which Paul clearly did not yet know, represents only one tradition, and not a uniform one at that. Yet all the statements agree without exception that Jesus' resurrection and exaltation as Lord, an event which men practiced in the ways of the world could hardly credit, much less anticipate, was actually experienced by the disciples in spite of their incomprehension and doubt. Without this faith not a single item in the Jesus tradition would have come down to us. Thus it is not a question of a few highlights and colors being borrowed from this faith and superimposed upon the tradition. Rather, the tradition in all its narratives and in all its variations is a confession and proclamation of Christ.

2. The Synoptic Gospels

There is a close relationship between Matthew, Mark, and
Luke, the so-called synoptic Gospels. Over large sections they
run parallel, and elsewhere at least two of the three agree;
particularly striking is the material common to Matthew and
Luke. In addition, each of the Gospels, especially Matthew
and Luke, has special traditions of its own—which is why
the three Gospels are of unequal length (Mark having six-
teen chapters, Matthew twenty-eight, and Luke twenty-four).
The various points of agreement and divergence are easily
traced in a "synopsis"—the term is derived from the Greek
word for "seeing together"—a reference work in which the
texts are printed in parallel columns.

THE SOURCES

After other solutions for explaining these agreements and
divergences had been tried and found inadequate, the "two-
source theory," first propounded and carefully documented
about a century ago, became generally accepted; it still holds
the field today. According to this theory, Mark is our earliest

Gospel; it forms the basis of the other two "major" Gospels and is embedded in them. In addition to their use of Mark, both Matthew and Luke make independent use of a second source; this is shown by the many individual sayings and groups of sayings, not found in Mark, which they have in common.

With the one exception of the story of the centurion (Matt. 8:5 ff.; Luke 7:1 ff.), this common tradition consists almost entirely of dominical sayings, sayings of the Lord. It contains no miracles, no conflict stories, and, most importantly, no passion or Easter narratives. For this reason this second source of Matthew and Luke is generally referred to among scholars as the "sayings source" or "Q" (from *Quelle,* the German word for "source").

There are strong arguments for the common assumption of the chronological priority of Mark (Matthew having previously been assumed to be the earliest Gospel). They may be listed as follows:

1. With almost negligible exceptions, all the narrative material in Mark is to be found in the other two synoptics, or at least in one of them.

2. Again, Mark's order of events is generally followed by the others. Not everywhere, of course, but whenever all three fail to agree, at least one of the other two nearly always agrees with Mark. And where there is a deviation (which by and large happens more frequently with Matthew than with Luke), it can usually be explained in terms of the exigencies of composition and as an inevitable consequence of the evangelist's need to combine the Marcan material with other traditions.

3. Finally, the far-reaching if not slavish agreement in wording is an important indication.

This two-source theory put an end to the older theory, sometimes revived even today, that Mark is a later work consisting of excerpts from Matthew and Luke, or an abbreviated version of the other two. Such a theory is impossible because it would not explain why Mark selected what he did and why he left out so much other material from Matthew and Luke. Why, for instance, would Mark have ignored Luke's Sermon on the Plain (Luke 6:20 ff.) or Matthew's Sermon on the Mount (Matt. 5–7), numerous parables of the kingdom (Matt. 13), the Lord's Prayer (Matt. 6:9 ff.; Luke 11:2 ff.), and many other passages? The same argument tells equally against the possibility that Matthew used Luke or vice versa. Here again we seek in vain for an explanation of the omissions.

For the reasons indicated we are no longer justified in speaking of the first plank in the two-source theory—the priority of Mark—as a mere hypothesis. It leaves plenty of questions unanswered. But we need not go into them here, and anyway they represent no serious challenge to the theory as such. Seldom does it happen, as here, that the historian is in the happy position of being able constantly to use as a control an earlier source still extant in a tolerably complete literary form.

Here we would list a few examples from the sayings source as we encounter it in Luke, which is generally considered the more original version (the parallel passages of course being found in Matthew): the Sermon on the Plain, Luke 6:20 ff., which in Matthew 5–7 is combined with further sayings material to form the Sermon on the Mount; Jesus' discourse on John the Baptist, Luke 7:18 ff.; the missionary charge, Luke 10:2 ff.; the woes on the Galilean cities and the cry of jubilation, Luke 10:13 ff., 21 ff.; the teaching on prayer, Luke 11:2 ff., 9 ff.; and the sayings about confession and discipleship, Luke 12:2 ff., and about anxiety and riches, Luke 12:22 ff.; 14:26 f. In addition there are a number of parables, such as the great supper, Luke 14:16 ff., and the lost sheep, Luke 15:1 ff.

The characteristics and peculiarities of this second source are more difficult to determine than those of Mark. There are so many parallels between Matthew and Luke that we can be confident that such a source existed. What we do not know is how far it had already acquired a fixed literary form. One thing is certain: it must have been quite different from the Gospel of Mark. Q was certainly not a gospel in the sense that Mark is. The way Q is used in Matthew and Luke shows that both evangelists treated it with more freedom and independence than they treated Mark. This is true both of its wording and its sequence of materials.

Mark and Q by no means exhaust the sources of the synoptic tradition. Even Mark has special material, though it is confined to three pericopes (4:26 ff.; 7:32 ff.; 8:22 ff.). Matthew has more special material, and Luke the most, covering both the earthly ministry and Easter narratives as well as the considerable material he has inserted within the Marcan framework. Here are some examples.

The special Matthean material contains numerous parables of the kingdom (13:14 ff., 36 ff., 44 ff., 47 ff.; 18:23 ff.; 20:1 ff.; 21:28 ff.; 25:1 ff., 31 ff.); the story of Peter walking on the water (14:28 ff.); and the famous "You are Peter" saying (16:16 ff.).

The special Lucan material includes the miraculous draft of fishes and the call of Peter (5:1 ff.); the widow's son at Nain (7:11 ff.); the parables of the fig tree (13:1 ff.), the importunate friend (11:5 ff.), and the unjust judge (18:1

ff.); the parables of the lost coin (15:8 ff.), the prodigal son (15:11 ff.), and the unjust steward (16:1 ff.); the healing of the ten lepers (17:11 ff.); and the story of Zacchaeus (19:1 ff.). In addition there are the illustrative stories of the good Samaritan (10:29 ff.), the rich fool (12:13 ff.), the rich man and Lazarus (16:19 ff.), and the Pharisee and the publican (18:9 ff.).

Many attempts have been made to organize this extensive and valuable special material into more or less connected sources, but they have not led to any generally accepted result. This means that literary and source criticism generally has not gotten beyond the two-source theory. It recognizes that oral tradition continued to flow in a broad stream, independently as well as within the literarily fixed tradition.

THE EARLIEST JESUS TRADITION

On the whole the results of earlier literary criticism have survived their ordeal by fire. They afford an initial insight into the process by which the Gospels came into being. But the superstructure which the older critics erected upon this foundation has not stood up, because they misunderstood the peculiarity, character, and purpose of the tradition. Without hesitation, they classified the Gospels in the same literary genre as other historical works of antiquity. They thought it was possible to reconstruct a fairly accurate biography of Jesus. One fact, of course, had to be taken into consideration. The evangelists were not trained historians, and popular tradition is always subject to change in the process of transmission. Something gets dropped at one point, something else added at another, and there is often a tendency toward legendary accretion. It cannot be denied that there are plenty of examples of this sort of thing in the Gospels.

Yet none of these considerations does justice to the Gospels. The fact is that the Gospels, not only the first three but to an even greater degree the fourth, are unique in ancient literature. They cannot be classified with the great works of such Greek and Roman historians as Thucydides, Polybius, and Tacitus, or with such contemporary biographies as Suetonius's *Lives of the Caesars* (ca. A.D. 70–140) and the much-esteemed biographies of Plutarch (ca. A.D. 45–125). Nor does the category of "memoirs" (of the apostles) fit them, a term already in vogue and applied to the Gospels by the Christian author Justin Martyr, who died about 165.

One of the first differences that strikes us between the Gospels and these other works is that the individuality of the evangelists hardly ever comes to the fore. It is significant that all of the Gospels are anonymous. The traditional names Matthew, Mark, Luke, and John cannot be traced back further than the second century. By this time there was an obvious concern to guarantee the tradition by attributing it to a known figure like one of the twelve (Matthew, John, and the apocryphal gospels of Peter, Thomas, and Philip) or to one of their assistants (Mark, Luke). Of the canonical gospels the one which comes closest to the work of an ancient historian is Luke. This can be seen from the preface (Luke 1:1–4) as well as from some features in its portrait of Jesus. Yet on the whole such instances are rare. The Jesus tradition simply would not fit that kind of narration. Thus even the third Gospel keeps more or less within the same framework as the others (see pp. 62 ff.).

More important, it is surprising that the Gospels show so little—or even no—interest in the historical personality of their "hero." There is nothing about Jesus' social or family background, the experiences of his youth, his talents, education, and development, his character, or even what he looked like. True, the author of the *Jesus-Report* (see above, p. 18) does describe—literally hair by hair—the appearance of "Jesus the Jew." But what he says is based on an obscure letter supposedly written by one of Pilate's superiors. In this way Lehmann tries to create the impression that he is dealing with assured facts, uncontaminated by Christian tradition. But he forgets to add that this dubious document is a late Christian forgery, probably as late as the twelfth century. It was an attempt of "pious fantasy" to describe the appearance of Jesus in accordance with contemporary taste, the kind of attempt that is familiar to us from countless religious pictures. Popular teaching records details of a highly imaginative kind. But that only confirms the strong influence of the traditional though erroneous impression that the Gospels are straightforward biographies.

To be sure, the Gospels do have something to say about Jesus' parents, even his family tree (Matt. 1; Luke 3), his trade (Mark 6:3) and that of his father (Matt. 13:55), and his brothers and sisters (Mark 6:3). But such details are scanty, and without exception they are devoid of biographical interest. It was left to legend to supply the need for biographical information. To some extent this has happened even within the canonical gospels, especially in the infancy narratives of Matthew and Luke. There is a rank outgrowth of it in the apocryphal gospels, but even there the interest is hardly biographical.

The further observations to be made at this point grow out of the more recent study of the Gospels. They are of far-reaching importance, although we have only gradually come to appreciate that fact. At first glance they appear to be merely formal in nature. Nonetheless they enable us to push our inquiry back behind the Gospels and their sources, and to catch a clear glimpse of the Jesus tradition while it was still in the oral stage. This inquiry into the preliterary tradition may sound like a foolhardy and hopeless enterprise. Historians have an ancient maxim to the effect that what cannot be documented does not exist (*quod non est in actis, non est in re*). The fear is that such a path is bound to lead into the unknown, into a jungle of unsupported speculation. Such fears, however, are unfounded in this instance, for everything that is to be said here can be read from the biblical texts. Our inquiry in fact leads us toward the texts and not away from them. In its essentials the procedure is generally accessible to everyone; it does not require any special scholarly equipment. The best approach is simply to use a "synopsis" (see above, p. 25). As is so often the case, all that is required is to keep one's eyes open, take note of a few facts, and reflect upon them. The reader need not be afraid of being caught up in a dispute between the pundits which may be either of no interest to him or perhaps beyond his depth.

Let us begin with a simple and obvious fact. The synoptic tradition consists of many self-contained units of material. Each unit has a clear beginning and an equally clear ending. Every scene and group of sayings stands by itself and does not depend on what precedes or follows. There is hardly ever a cross-reference to anything that comes before or after. On the rare occasions where such a reference does occur, it generally stands out like a foreign body from the rest of the context. Anyone can observe at a glance how the individual "pericopes" stand on their own feet.

It is true that the Gospels create the impression of a consecutive story. But this is due to the evangelists' use of repeated indications of time and place ("after . . . ," "and when

Jesus . . . ," "at evening . . ."), and sometimes of short stereotyped connecting links and introductory sentences, to join the separate pieces of tradition to one another. But the texts do not offer a real segment of reconstructible history. The chronological and topographical notices are far too meager and uniform for that. They bear no relation to what the pericopes actually contain, and they often differ from one Gospel to another. In fact, the evangelists—like the earlier collectors before them—handle them with surprising freedom, as a device for grouping the materials available from the tradition. The authors of the two major synoptic Gospels (Matthew and Luke) even treated Mark the same way, despite the fact that they used his Gospel as their source and followed his outline pretty faithfully. Wherever they wanted to add similar material from another tradition, or thought it advisable for some other reason, they broke up the Marcan order without any ado or abandoned it completely.

Of course it is entirely possible that credible reminiscences, tied to a particular situation, have been preserved in some of these notices. Every case has to be considered on its own merits, although it is often difficult to be certain. The only thing that matters is that we should grasp the real purpose behind these notices. They are redactional rather than chronological. Earlier interpreters used to pay a good deal of attention to such notices. They even deduced from the accidental sequence of the scenes the psychological feelings of Jesus, his disciples, or his hearers on any given occasion. But that sort of thing regularly ended up in miserably sentimental fantasizing. Anyone who listens to a sermon in church can safely go to sleep if the preacher expatiates in that fashion. He may be sure that he will not miss anything that is really vital to the text.

From such observations we learn to distinguish between the bedrock of the tradition and the adaptations it has undergone in later redaction, and this sharpens our eye for the real point of the text itself. Of course, this also means that we shall drop many of the historical and pragmatic questions which earlier generations spent so much effort and ingenuity in trying to solve. We shall have to leave such questions open, be more critical in our answers, and attach less importance to them.

Let us take a few examples. Where, for instance, should we look for the mountain of the temptation (Matt. 4 and parallel), the site of the Sermon on the Mount (Matt. 5:1), the mountain of the transfiguration (Mark 9 and parallels), or the mountain of the great missionary charge (Matt. 28)? None of these places can be pinpointed on a map. Nor does it matter in the slightest whether Jesus was anointed at the beginning of his passion in Bethany near Jerusalem (Mark 14; Matt. 26; John 12) or on a much earlier occasion in Galilee when he was at supper in the house of a Pharisee (Luke 7:36 ff.). On the other hand, it is not unimportant that Luke uses the anointing scene to introduce the parable of the two debtors. Or take the question about the greatest commandment. Luke alone places it not among the Jerusalem conflict stories, where the other Gospels have it, but in his long "travel section" (Luke 9:51–18:14). Here the scribe's question receives a conclusive answer in the story of the good Samaritan (10:30 ff.).

Examples like these could easily be multiplied. They show how much the emphasis in scholarship has shifted. It is no longer a question of whether or when something happened in the life of Jesus, or of what he actually said. The question now is, What did the original narrators and the later collectors mean when they used these particular units of tradition, and what are they still saying to us today? Only by asking this question can we do them justice. Any other way we misrepresent them.

One of the characteristics of the earliest oral tradition which can still be clearly discerned is that it follows definite forms and fixed laws of transmission. These forms are not selected at random by the individual narrators according to their own predilections, talents, or tastes, but are molded in a way that transcends individuality and is entirely determined by content. They are not just empty forms, nor are they to be regarded primarily from an aesthetic or artistic point of view.

Even the authentic sayings of Jesus are couched in such forms. His prophetic sayings about the coming of the kingdom of God and the hour of salvation have a structure of their own. The wisdom sayings have a different structure. They are pointed and concise, expressing with the utmost simplicity a universal truth. They do not require the learning of a scribe but appeal directly to the understanding of the audience. Again, take many of Jesus' parables, or the sayings about the folly and needlessness of anxiety (Matt. 6:25 ff. and parallel). Or take the large number of sayings which are either similar or identical to those in Jewish collections, or are even paralleled in collections of proverbs outside the Bible. Still another type is found in Jesus' sayings about the commandments and the will of God. These occur in conflict stories, where he argues with his Jewish opponents. Then there are the antitheses in the Sermon on the Mount ("You have heard . . . but I say to you . . ."). All of these forms were preserved by the later tradition, which also developed similar sayings of its own (cf. the differences between the

Sermon on the Plain in Luke 6 and the Sermon on the Mount in Matthew 5–7).

Many of Jesus' sayings are handed down in the form of anecdotes. They are introduced with a brief description of the situation, and sometimes expanded into little dialogues, or apothegms as they are called in Greek. The narrative elements may change in the process of expansion, like the groupings of the material as a whole. What never changes— at least not radically—is the saying of Jesus itself, which contains the point and usually closes the scene.

Another group in the tradition consists of stories about Jesus, the stories of his healings and miracles. They too are generally constructed according to fixed laws, laws which may be studied also in the stories about other great miracle-workers, especially in the pagan and Hellenistic world. A typical feature of the healings, for example, is the introduction, which describes the patient's distress, the duration of the illness and its symptoms, the unsuccessful and expensive attempts of the physicians to cure it, and the heckling or wailing of the bystanders. Then comes the effective word of the great miracle-worker, often in a mysterious foreign language ("Ephphatha," Mark 7:34; "Talitha cumi," Mark 5:41) and sometimes accompanied by a healing gesture (he took him by the hand; touched the tongue of the dumb; put a mixture of spittle and clay on the eyes of the blind). Then the cure: the evil spirit leaves the demoniac, the lame man gets up, the blind man sees trees and people, the person healed demonstrates the effect of the miracle before the bystanders, who then burst forth in astonishment and praise. As these stories are constantly retold—a process which can often be traced from one Gospel to another, and still more in later legend—a tendency to stylistic embellishment can be observed. The unique features of the situation are described in greater breadth, and the participants acquire names or even an individual profile.

A special area in which the tendencies and laws of popular transmission operate is that of legend, which will be briefly mentioned here. Legend plays some part in the New Testament tradition of Jesus, though not a dominant one. In modern usage legend is regarded as the product of pious fantasy, usually in contrast to historical report. But that does not do it justice. It can have reference to historical actualities. Nobody would seriously deny Jesus' birth, his baptism by John, his last meal with his disciples, or his crucifixion. But the question has to do with how the story of such events is narrated, and with what interest, and to what purpose. The answer is that the narrator's interest was not in writing history but in the holiness or exemplary piety of certain figures. This is true not only with respect to Jesus but also with respect to others like the holy men and women who appear in the infancy narratives of Matthew and Luke (Zechariah and Elizabeth, Mary and Joseph, Simeon and Anna), and to certain of the apostles in Acts. Here we find legendary traits in some of the details, or even entire scenes which go beyond the limits of the "historical" with their various miracles, angels, and signs from heaven.

Again, some stories—e.g., the baptism of Jesus or the institution of the Lord's Supper—are unconsciously assimilated to the liturgical customs of the later community. Also typical is the similarity between Matthew's infancy narrative and the Old Testament and Jewish legends about Moses. This also explains the considerable variations in the Gethsemane scene and the crucifixion, as well as the Easter and ascension stories.

In some cases we may well ask whether we are justified in speaking of legends or legendary embellishments at all. Even some of Jesus' sayings, like those which speak of his mission, his exalted status, and his fate, to say nothing of entire stories like the baptism, the temptation, Peter's confession, the transfiguration, the triumphal entry, and the trial before the Sanhedrin, are—whatever the historical substratum may be—so strongly colored by the community's faith in Christ and by the way the believers reproduce the incident in question, that the expression "legend" hardly seems adequate here. In distinction to the older and simpler pieces of tradition, whose chief purpose is to awaken faith in Jesus, these stories are much more thoroughly impregnated with Christian faith and confession. But of course between legend and faith there are no hard and fast boundaries.

Certain characteristics of the Jesus tradition are particularly striking. Let us call special attention to three of them which belong closely together.

First, there is the focus upon the person of Jesus. None of the individual scenes has the lengthy introduction we usually expect in the writing of history. Minor characters suddenly appear on the stage and as a rule disappear just as suddenly into the obscurity from which they came. None of them receives—as in Homer—any permanent characterization. The New Testament records concentrate upon Jesus' word and deed and proclaim who he is, not just who he was.

Second, the gospel stories are beamed particularly toward the person addressed. It would be easy to ask questions out of idle curiosity: How did John the Baptist react to Jesus' answer, which his disciples brought back to him in prison (Matt. 11:2–6 and parallel)? What happened to the three would-be disciples when they heard what it would cost to follow Jesus (Luke 9:57–62)? Did Peter take to heart Jesus' harsh rejoinder, "Get behind me, Satan," when he tried to deflect him from the way of the cross (Mark 8:33)? Or what became of all the persons Jesus healed, and of the disciples and opponents who turn up all over the place? Almost invariably such questions remain unanswered. Only later legend was interested in what happened afterwards to Pilate, to the centurion at the cross, or to Nicodemus. The participants in any particular scene are unimportant. What matters is the response of those who hear or read the story.

Third, there is a connection between the accounts and the faith and life of the believing community. No part of the tradition was preserved merely for its own sake, because of the interest its details held for the conscientious reporter. It was preserved because in one degree or another the story it told was of vital concern to the life and faith of Jesus' community and should remain so. This is not to say that every detail is only a subsequent reflection of faith or a product of imagination. Such total skepticism is entirely out of place. Rather, we have every reason to trust the simple and practiced memories of the earliest disciples. After all, their minds had not been atrophied by printer's ink and the mass media which surfeit us every day.

Yet we should not underestimate the influence which the faith and life of the post-Easter community had on the formation of the Jesus tradition from the very beginning. Obviously, there was a good deal of give-and-take. The early church needed the tradition in order to be and remain certain of its faith in Jesus as the bringer of salvation. It had to hold its own in debate with its Jewish and pagan neighbors, and to defend itself from internal dangers. It needed directions for its practical life, help in prayer, answers to fresh questions, and clear-cut subject matter and guidelines for evangelistic preaching and catechetical instruction. But on the other hand, the particular situation of the community, its specific traditions, views, and modes of thought in various places, had a strong effect on the Jesus tradition, which was far from being uniformly shaped. The community incorporated its own experiences, questions, and insights into the tradition. If we are to understand the origins and peculiarities of the Jesus tradition aright, we must be constantly aware of the way it was interwoven with the vital expressions and requirements and questions of the community which constituted its *Sitz im Leben,* its creative milieu.

Again, all this is not just guesswork. What we have said is actually borne out by the first three Gospels. They all contain unmistakable traces of the oral tradition which preceded them. Matthew, as we shall show, wrote his Gospel for a community which in many ways had a different structure from that of Mark before him, and Luke again is different from the other two, to say nothing of John. A comparison shows that the three synoptics not only assimilated different traditions but also transmitted them differently. This is all the more remarkable since Matthew and Luke, as we have seen, had at hand in addition to Mark a second source which was more or less fixed in form and followed their primary source with considerable care, though also with a certain freedom. The composition of the Gospels thus represents the beginning rather than the end of a regulative process. The variety of tradition stands not at the end but at the beginning of the development. Luke claimed as much in the prologue to his Gospel and left us in no doubt about it (Luke 1:1–4). At the same time the evangelists did not deprive the earliest tradition of its vitality and idiosyncrasies but actually carried them further. Had they not done so, they would have defeated their own purpose. In this sense every evangelist, as Matthew so happily expressed it, is like "a householder who can produce from his store both the new and the old" (13:52).

What we have said thus far can be summed up as follows: The Jesus tradition which has been collected and processed in the Gospels represents a unique blend of narrative and confession, of stories about Jesus and witness of the community which believed in him. There is nothing like it in ancient literature. Indeed, it is really narrative *as* confession, faith proclaimed *as* a story about Jesus. The two form an inseparable unity. To the early Christians Jesus was not just a tragic figure of the past who ended his life on the cross, but one who through his resurrection became the living, present, and coming Lord. This does not mean that he was replaced by a mythical figure. He was still the same Jesus as before. We recall what we said earlier about kerygma and creed: "Jesus Christ is *Lord*" and "The Lord is *Jesus*" (Phil. 2:11; 1 Cor. 12:3). Thus the story of his past never lost its contemporary relevance but acquired ever fresh significance.

TYPES OF THE CHRIST-MESSAGE

How did the Jesus tradition with all its many facets become a single whole? Everything we know suggests that Mark was the first to compose a written gospel. But before Mark there must have been smaller collections which developed independently and continued to exist side by side with Mark and after him. These earlier collections of material, however, can no longer be clearly identified as literary sources. Indeed they probably should not be envisaged as entities of that kind at all. They are only various types of oral tradition

circulating independently of one another, the earliest forms
to crystallize, so to speak.

Jesus' Teaching with Authority

One of the earliest collections of this type we have already
encountered in the form of the sayings source. From this
source Matthew and Luke drew an appreciable amount of
their common tradition (see above, pp. 27 f.). The most
striking thing about this sayings source is that it contains no
miracle stories apart from the story of the centurion at Caper-
naum (Matt. 8:5 ff.; Luke 7:1 ff.), although it knows of
Jesus' mighty works (Luke 10:13 ff.; 11:20 ff., 24 ff.). Nor
does it include a passion narrative, or even the slightest hint
of one. All the more abundant is the stock of Jesus' sayings,
some of them unquestionably very primitive, others compara-
tively late. There is his authoritative message about the dawning kingdom of God (Matt. 12:25 ff., 38 ff., 43 ff.); his call
to discipleship, a call which involved both promise and de-
mand (Luke 9:57 ff.); and his call to courageous testimony
(Luke 12:2 ff.), even when it means the breach of the
closest family ties (Luke 14:26 f.). Particularly forceful is
the call for decision in face of the new age which is just
dawning with Jesus' coming, although the will of God proclaimed in the Old Testament law is never questioned (Matt.
4:4 ff.). But Jesus, who has already appeared in earthly form
and will come again as Son of man to judge the world, is
greater than Jonah and Solomon (Matt. 12:41–42). The
contrast between him and "this generation," to say nothing
of the legalistic piety of the scribes, is a glaring one. As the
Son, "everything is entrusted to [him] by [his] Father,"
and he reveals it to whom he will—not to the learned and
wise but to the simple (Luke 10:21 f.).

As is immediately obvious, this collection of sayings is no pious attempt to preserve the heritage of one now dead, nor a series of timeless ethical maxims or sound advice for daily living. Jesus' word spoken in the past is still alive and relevant, delivered by his accredited messengers. It calls for decision and offers salvation. Yet there is no discernible christological reflection about him as the bringer of salvation, nothing even about his end on the cross. All the same, these sayings reflect a strong faith in Jesus' messiahship. Despite their complete silence about his death, the certainty of Easter is unmistakable.

Mark could hardly have known the sayings source (Q), yet his Gospel also contains sayings material of a similar kind, though less of it. Sometimes he records sayings identical with those in Q. There are also rudimentary collections of sayings (cf. especially the collection of parables in Mark 4).

Collections of sayings—the earliest form of the Jesus tradition—continued to exist independently even after the compilation of our Gospels. This may be seen from numerous quotations in the early fathers. But more importantly, we now have definitive proof in the Gospel of Thomas, a document preserved in its entirety in a Coptic version composed in the second century, and discovered only in 1945. The Gospel of Thomas contains 114 sayings of Jesus. As in Q, they are loosely joined together, and there are only sayings—no deeds, no passion, no Easter stories. These sayings all purport to be words of the living Christ; they include several parallels to Q.

But all the way through, the meaning of the sayings has undergone a curious shift. In the Gospel of Thomas Jesus himself figures exclusively as the mediator of a revelation from heaven, devoid of all earthly or human characteristics.

In this capacity he delivers gnostic and dualistic teachings to an eclectic circle of disciples, calling them to renounce and withdraw from this alien material world and to prepare themselves for the new, eternal, transcendent world of light from which they come. Thus the Gospel of Thomas exhibits tendencies which set it apart from an unadulterated collection of Jesus' sayings, tendencies which, despite the similarity in form, are not found at all in Q.

The Mighty Works of Jesus

The healings, exorcisms, and other miracles, which are transmitted in abundance, particularly in Mark, form an entirely different type of Jesus tradition, quite independent of the sayings. As we have already observed, these units of material are very similar in form to Hellenistic-Gentile stories about mighty miracle-workers (see above, pp. 36 f.). There is no need here to discuss the historicity of such deeds in detail. Nobody will deny that Jesus had powers which enabled him to heal those who were plagued by evil spirits. His contemporaries had no doubt that such powers were miraculous. But it is equally obvious that in early Christianity many miracles, individual motifs, and entire scenes from the stories of other miracle-workers were transferred to Jesus in order to proclaim him as the true source of help.

In the New Testament stories about Jesus there is much that comes from contemporary folklore and has been left in the crude state in which it was originally found. This does not seem to have troubled the early Christians. There are coarse traits, sometimes amusing, as in the story of the Gerasene swine. Two thousand pigs rushed headlong down the cliff and into the sea, driven by the raging demon from behind, and the whole lot drowned (Mark 5:1–19). Or again, take the incredible amount of wine at the wedding at Cana, a miracle which is unwittingly confirmed by the steward with his jocular remark to the bridegroom (John 2:1 ff.). Then there are plenty of examples of primitive magic (Mark 5:28 ff.) and the attribution of sickness to demons, a popular notion in the contemporary world. Such things simply cannot be explained away or made plausible by rationalistic interpretation in the hope of preserving their historicity. The primary purpose of the storytellers was to describe the incredible as a vehicle for the "epiphany" of the divine miracle-worker.

Of course there is more to the New Testament miracle stories than that. Equally unmistakable is the way they are used as vehicles for the genuine proclamation of Christ. They portray the strong compassion of Jesus for the oppressed, the outcast, those whom society has condemned as unclean, the lepers and the demoniacs. It is significant that, of the seventeen miracles related in Mark, thirteen are exorcisms, to say nothing of the generalized summaries where exorcisms are especially emphasized (1:32 ff.; 3:7 ff.; 6:53 ff.). The narrator is not concerned to glorify Jesus as just one wonder-worker among others, whose exploits excel the rest. He is *the* Holy One of God (Mark 1:24), *the* Son of God (Mark 3:11), and the "stronger one" who binds the strong man (Satan) and wrests his prey from him (Mark 3:27).

In line with this is the emphasis on the dawn of salvation. In the "choric ending" of the healing of the deaf-mute (Mark 7:31–37), the crowd cries out: "All that he does, he does well . . . he even makes the deaf hear and the dumb speak"—an obvious allusion to the creation story (Gen.

1:31). The same point comes out in the way Matt. 11:5 takes up the prophecy of Isa. 35:5 f.

Another example of the same sort of thing is the way in which many of the stories as they now stand are permeated with allusions to the praise of God. Without losing their literal meaning, they acquire a symbolic significance, even if that was not there from the outset. Examples of this may be seen in the stilling of the storm (Mark 4:35 ff.) and the healing of the blind (Mark 10:46 ff. and elsewhere, the clearest example being John 9:1 ff.).

More than that, where we can compare one text with another we observe not only the tendency to novelistic embroidery already noted (see above, p. 37), but even more often the reverse tendency to suppress unique episodes in favor of typical examples, and the strong preference for the motif of faith ("Your faith has cured you," Mark 5:34; cf. Matt. 15:28). Thus the individual story becomes a transparent vehicle. Stories are transformed into a single story, or, to be precise, into the story of Jesus interpreted in the light of faith.

Obviously, this type of Jesus tradition constitutes an independent form of the proclamation of Christ. It focuses upon the authority of Jesus displayed in his deeds. There is nothing to suggest that this type of proclamation, taken by itself, was oriented toward Jesus' suffering and death. This is true both of the individual episodes, which contain no reference to the suffering and death, and of the shorter or longer collections, such as the rudimentary collection underlying Mark 4:35–5:43 and "the signs source" in John, a special source where the miraculous traits are remarkably heightened.

Nor can we assume that there was a close connection between the miracle stories in their original form and the teaching material. Of course it is significant that in the process of transmission these two have frequently been brought together.

It would be too crude and quite unpardonable to write off the miracle stories of the Jesus tradition as a pagan accretion simply on the ground of their unquestionable affinities with the miracle stories of antiquity. Yet it cannot be denied that there is a strange ambivalence in this genre of the tradition. It might just as easily have developed in a pagan direction instead of becoming a vehicle for the authentic Christian message. The seeds of heresy were latent in it from the start. We can see this quite early on in the passionate struggle in which Paul was engaged with his opponents at Corinth, who obviously took Christ to be a divine man of the pagan type and accordingly expected his apostle to perform similar demonstrations of divine power (see below, p. 101).

The Fate of Jesus

Thus far we have hardly mentioned Jesus' passion and resurrection. This is because neither type of the earliest tradition—neither his words nor his deeds—show any perceptible influence of the passion kerygma. Yet there can be no doubt that the community was intensely concerned with Jesus' end from the very outset. It was no accident that the separate pericopes of the passion were soon combined into a connected story, though this did not happen to the Easter stories for some time.

According to the synoptists, the passion started with the decision of the Sanhedrin to put Jesus to death. It continued with his anointing, his betrayal by Judas, and the Last Supper with his disciples at Passover time. Then came Gethsemane, the arrest, the arraignment before the Sanhedrin and Pilate, and the mocking. Finally it culminated with Jesus' crucifixion, death, and burial (Mark 14–15; Matt. 26–27; Luke 22–23).

In John 18–19 the continuous narrative does not begin until the arrest. Yet despite certain differences in detail the specific instances of agreement between the four Gospels are far more frequent in the passion narrative than elsewhere. Also the disproportionately large number of episodes—involving as they do the events of a single week—is just as noticeable in John as in the synoptics. The reason for this can easily be understood when we recall the importance of the end of Jesus' earthly history for the message and faith of the earliest community (see above, pp. 20 f.).

Yet the passion story is not modeled on any particular formula of confession or catechesis. It is not that a creed has been transformed into a historical account. The New Testament contains a wide variety of brief summaries of the faith. But none of them provides as it were *the* theological pattern for the gospel accounts of the passion. Let us take a few examples. The important phrase in 1 Cor. 15:3–5, "for our sins," never becomes the theme of the passion stories (with one exception, the cup-word in Matt. 26:29). Nor do the central motifs of the pre-Pauline hymn in Phil. 2:6–11—humiliation, exaltation, *Kyrios* ("Lord")—become key words in the passion narratives. Again, the contrast between rejection and vindication which figures in the kerygmatic speeches of Acts, "You have killed him. . . . God raised him from the dead" (Acts 2:23–24; 3:15), is much too formal to exhaust the burden of the narrative. Even the three prophecies of suffering which have been put into the mouth of Jesus (Mark 8:31; 9:31; 10:33 f.), the third of which contains a complete summary of the passion and Easter stories, are only occasionally echoed in Mark 14–15 (14:21, 41 and parallels). The great christological theme of the suffering and rising Son of man is entirely lacking.

The uncritical reader may not think that there is anything particularly important in these observations. But they are not unimportant for our purposes. They confirm the fact that the passion narratives cannot be forced into a theological mold. Generally they tell a story, nothing but a story, and one has to search behind the narrative as a whole and in each individual text for any deeper thought. All the same, they are not a straightforward report about Jesus. Rather, they are permeated with reflections and motifs both theological and christological. This is proven by the frequent quotations from Scripture and allusions to the prophets and psalms, from the entry into Jerusalem and the cleansing of the Temple (Mark 11) to the moment of Jesus' death. These citations testify unmistakably that the end of Jesus with all its horror was not a confused tragedy but the fulfillment of the purpose and will of God. Thus in every scene Jesus stands in striking contrast to all the human actors. He is condemned for blasphemy and treason by his opponents, betrayed by his disciples, denied and forsaken. Yet in the depth of his dereliction (Mark 15:34; Matt. 27:46) he is still the true "King of the Jews" and "Son of God" (Mark 14:60; 15:39).

The last words from the cross vary considerably in all four Gospels. And the picture of Jesus' last hour is drawn with characteristic differences in each Gospel. But this shows the varieties of expression which faith could give to the mission of Jesus and his story. His end does not contradict his mission. They were both of a piece.

None of the passion stories would be conceivable without the certainty of Easter faith. Each story expresses this in its own way. Yet none should be labeled with the superficial slogan "through the night to light" (*per aspera ad astra*).

That is evident from the way the Easter tradition, in marked contrast to the passion tradition, fans out in so many directions in the Gospels, the one exception being the story of the empty tomb, in which the Gospels differ only in slight details.

Finally, there is another point worth noting. The passion stories hardly ever refer to Jesus' miracles, the only exception being Mark 15:31 and parallels. The miracle stories obviously belong to a different branch of the Jesus tradition. Nor is there any noticeable influence of the sayings tradition. Only Luke has incorporated a few sayings in the passion sequence (22:24–30). Here again the individual complexes of the earliest tradition are clearly distinguishable from one another. The passion tradition, like the others, grew up independently, with the earthly history of Jesus prior to his suffering curiously overshadowed.

MARK—MATTHEW—LUKE

The Son of God (Mark)

In the canon and usage of the church Matthew has occupied first place from early times. By contrast, the Gospel of Mark has led a somewhat shadowy existence. It is noticeable how few excerpts from Mark are used in the traditional Sunday pericopes. Yet Mark's importance for the history of Christianity can hardly be overrated. We know very little of how the Gospel of Mark came to be written. Like the other Gospels, it is anonymous. The later tradition about authorship is not earlier than the second century and is historically worthless. According to this tradition, Mark was once a travel companion of Paul and became the secretary and interpreter of Peter. The tradition is obviously intended to insure an indirect apostolic authority for the Gospel. In all probability the Gospel of Mark was compiled for Greeks in a Christian community somewhere in the east (Syria?) about the time of the Judeo-Roman war (ca. A.D. 70).

In Mark's Gospel the Jesus tradition, previously handed down in oral form, appears for the first time in the shape of a book. Historically this was an event of enormous importance. Yet we should divest ourselves of modern associations at this point. Mark probably had no intention of creating a sensational innovation. Like his predecessors and successors, all he wanted to do was to collect and preserve the scattered fragments of the Jesus tradition which were circulating in oral form, and make available the saving message of the crucified and risen Lord. This is exactly what early Hellenistic Christian preachers had been doing for a long time. That this is how Mark wanted his work understood is expressed in the very first sentence, which forms the title to the whole work: "the gospel of Jesus Christ" (1:1). Here and wherever else the word "gospel" occurs in Mark (8:35; 10:29; 13:10), it has the same meaning as it had for Paul. The gospel is the message of salvation, directed to the hearer always with the same unchangeable content (see above, pp. 20 ff.). It is not a new literary genre.

But there is something new. Included in this gospel is the story of the earthly Jesus prior to Good Friday and Easter. It would be wrong to understand this process as no more than an expansion of the traditional kerygma, or a historical supplement to it, reduced as the kerygma had been to the cross and resurrection. Mark's Gospel is not a mistaken attempt to impose the fixed form of the kerygma upon traditional materials basically alien to it.

The evangelist knows full well what he is doing and does a thorough job of it. He takes the various types of tradition and rivets them to the kerygma of the crucified and risen Lord, but at the same time anchors the kerygma firmly in the history of the earthly Jesus. For Mark, that history is certainly important and meaningful. It has its own specific places and times. Galilee is the first scene of Jesus' activity, which then widens out to include Phoenicia, Caesarea Philippi, and the Hermon range and the Decapolis east of the Sea of Galilee and the Jordan River (1–8). The later stages take us to Judea and Jerusalem (11–13), where Jesus meets his end (14–16). But these geographical areas have a deeper meaning. They mark first an initial period when Jesus teaches and works with authority away from the center of Judaism, in areas where the despised pagans lived and worked. As a result he makes enemies, and though he remains strangely hidden, the light of salvation shines forth. Then he appears openly, no longer hidden, and as the conflict reaches its climax, he meets his end. In this way Mark makes it clear, albeit only with broad strokes on his canvas, that what we have here is a real history, a history which embodies an event with a final, eschatological dimension.

The basic theology of Mark, like that of the other synoptists, may further be recognized in the way he uses the tradition that came his way. For a time, in reaction against the old quest of the historical Jesus, scholars concentrated on extracting little units of material and analyzing their forms. Inevitably, they paid little attention to the later "redaction." As we have seen, they had good reason for doing so. At first they regarded the synoptists merely as collectors who for the most part arranged their material in similar ways, though with occasional differences, and who in doing so had only very modest means at their disposal. In the meantime, however, it has been shown that each of the first three Gospels has a definite and highly individual theology of its own. This comes out in the way the evangelists select and arrange their material, in their choice of words and characteristic accents, and sometimes in sayings or connecting links they have freely composed themselves. This kind of study has led to most positive results. We are on sure ground when we compare parallels, e.g., Matthew and Luke with Mark or the Q material as reproduced by the two major evangelists. Yet it is true even of Mark, as for every type of collection of tradition prior to him, that he reproduces the earlier material in such a way as to update it for his own age.

It is characteristic of Mark, and significant, that after the programmatic introduction of his Gospel (1:1–15) and the calling of the first disciples (1:16–20), he closely coordinates Jesus' teachings and deeds in chapters 1–8 (through 8:26), both the words and the deeds being equally manifestations of the "power" of Jesus (1:21–28). The two kinds of traditional material alternate. Moreover, pieces from each are sometimes shaped in such a way as to comprise both teaching and deeds. This is notably the case with the healing of the paralytic (2:1–12), where the narrative is in the proper form of a miracle story, but has inserted into it a dispute, equally proper in form, between Jesus and the scribes over his power to forgive sins (vv. 6–10). Then there are healings narrated by Mark (3:1–5) and other evangelists which, in the eyes of the Jews, are blasphemous because they took place on the sabbath (cf. Luke 13:10 ff.; 14:1 ff.; John 5:9 ff.; 9:16 ff.). These too are proofs of his power in word and deed. The two belong together. "What is this? A new kind of teaching! He speaks with authority. When he gives orders, even the unclean spirits submit" (1:27).

In this way two quite different developments of the Jesus message, each with its own particular forms and laws, have been deliberately interwoven. The evangelist thus gives both lines of tradition their due. With his preaching of the kingdom, Jesus himself is the messenger of good news (1:14 f.). He delivers authoritative teaching and opposes the petrified piety of legalistic Judaism. He consorts with sinners and calls them, not the righteous, to the joy of repentance (2:13 ff.)—"fresh skins for new wine" (2:22). But no less is he victorious over the power of Satan and the dread forces of disease.

Mark also devoted much space to the miracle tradition. He certainly did not do so for want of better material. Of course he was a child of his age and accepted the reality of the stories without question. But they had a kerygmatic significance which we may find hard to understand. For a Christian, the deeds of Jesus are not the exploits of any ordinary miracle-worker. They had been baptized, as it were, long before Mark got hold of them. Yet, as we have seen, they were originally intended as immediate and direct epiphanies of the divine wonder-worker. But at this point the evangelist intervened quite forcefully—sometimes even violently—with the tradition, betraying his own hand clearly in turns of speech which break the continuity and imprint upon the material thoughts and motifs originally alien to it. Thus he attests his faith in the passion kerygma. This is the clue to the "messianic secret" so characteristic of Mark, a device which permeates the whole Gospel. Only in the cross and resurrection does the messiahship of Jesus or—more correctly, according to Mark—his divine sonship (8:31 ff.; 9:9) become apparent. To omit Jesus' end would be to falsify the message of salvation.

Mark expresses this through certain redactional devices which have the effect of putting a break in the story. An injunction to silence is repeatedly addressed to the demons, who are already aware of Jesus' true nature and recognize in him their invincible opponent (1:34; 3:12), and to the healed (1:44; 5:43; 7:26) and the disciples (8:30; 9:9). But this is not all. Jesus' message of the kingdom is fraught with the same secret and can be correctly understood only in the light of his end. Hence the curious notion that Jesus' parables, far from elucidating his preaching, have precisely the opposite effect. They produce misunderstanding and hardening in "those outside" (the "parable theory," 4:10–12).

The crucified and risen One is the Son of God! Of all Mark's christological titles this is the clearest and most important expression of his understanding of Christ. Other titles, like Messiah (*Christos*), Son of David, and the Holy One of God, take second place. Although the apocalyptic designation "Son of man" is of great importance, on the lips of Jesus himself it always points more to the manifold secret of his majesty: that already here on earth (2:10, 28) and in his suffering and rising (8:31; 9:9; 10:33, 45) and in his future coming to judge the world (8:38; 13:26; 14:62) he is the exalted One. On the other hand the title "the Son" also appears, in passages of a different type where there is a clear, summary confession of faith.

The most important statements of this sort occur at crucial points, at the beginning, in the middle, and at the end of the Gospel. Each is accompanied by supernatural or cosmic signs. In the baptism and transfiguration stories a voice from heaven proclaims Jesus as God's beloved Son (1:11; 9:7). At the foot of the cross the centurion confesses that Jesus is the Son of God (15:39). In a somewhat similar vein there are the utterances of his enemies—the cry of the demons (3:11 f.; 5:7) and the question of the high priest at the trial before the Sanhedrin, when Jesus responds to the charge of blasphemy with an unequivocal yes (14:61 f.). Nowhere in these passages is there any speculation about the supernatural birth of Jesus. They speak unanimously of his heavenly origin and the purpose of his mission all the way through to his end.

What meaning have the cross and resurrection for Jesus' divine sonship in Mark? Does the secrecy of the divine sonship with its constant pointing forward imply that Jesus on earth is not yet the Son of God, but only becomes so after his exaltation? As a matter of fact, this type of Christology was prevalent in some quarters in the early church. There can be no doubt that there was a good deal of fanatical enthusiasm after Jesus' resurrection. Many were convinced that the threshold of the aeons had already been crossed; the story of the earthly Jesus is finished, his cross has been annulled, and we are already living in the kingdom of God. Mark's tendency is just the reverse. But he never sacrifices the eschatological certainty, without which the whole of primitive Christianity would be unthinkable.

Rather, Mark's message is that the end has already dawned with the history of the earthly Jesus. Armed with the power of the Spirit, the Son of God speaks with authority and vanquishes the demons. Yet his authority and victory can only be discerned in the light of the cross. This is the climax of his mission, for he came not to be served but to serve and to offer his life for all (10:45). The resurrection of Jesus is not an escape from his earthly history into a mythical realm beyond. It does not negate or invalidate his death on the cross. Rather, his historical end—and not only that but the whole of his earthly work—now comes into its own. This is the full-scale, final battle between God and Satan (1:12 f.), initiated and executed in Jesus' mission, and to be consummated when he comes again in glory (8:38).

In this way the evangelist proclaims the history of Jesus as an eschatological event; his history is the end, but the end occurs in history. This is why Mark places the great apocalyptic discourse just before the passion (13). This device also achieves a second objective, namely, to instruct the church in the meaning of the time allotted to it on earth.

The same point is made, though in a different way, in the carefully articulated instructions to the disciples in 8:27–10:52. This section is one of several in which the shadow of the passion looms ever larger over Mark's presentation of Jesus' ministry on earth. In a series of advance notices fresh signals constantly recur (2:19 f.; 3:6). Then there are three places where passion predictions are combined with sayings on discipleship. Discipleship means being prepared for suffering and service (8:31 f., 34 ff.; 9:31 f., 33 ff.; 10:32 ff., 35 ff.). Until the Son of man comes in glory (8:38) the church's path will be difficult, though full of promise. For it is the way he trod while on earth.

In the earliest of the Gospels history and eschatology, authority and cross, God's appearance and his hiddenness stand side by side. The tension is kept at a maximum in contrapuntal fashion. Dibelius was quite right when he called Mark the "book of secret epiphanies."

The Teacher of the Church (Matthew)

As we have seen, Mark was the first to take the scattered fragments and different types of Jesus tradition and arrange them into a single whole, thus giving the tradition a contemporary and relevant interpretation and perpetuating it in book form. Mark's achievement quickly won recognition. This is shown by the Gospel of Matthew, also composed in Greek, a decade or two later than Mark.

Matthew incorporated Mark almost in its entirety, but revised it and added material from other sources (Q and the special Matthean material). Matthew's organization is masterly and impressive in its clarity. All this readily explains the high regard the church has had for Matthew's Gospel throughout its history, a regard which was reinforced by the erroneous opinion, originating in the first half of the second century, that this Gospel was the work of the tax collector who became a disciple of Jesus (9:9; 10:3). Matthew's was thus thought to be the earliest of the Gospels.

Matthew, as we have seen, is dependent on Mark. He is highly critical of the Pharisees, who became the unquestioned leaders of the Jewish community after the destruction of the Temple (A.D. 70). The church to which the evangelist belongs and for which he wrote was in an advanced stage of development. All of these considerations, as well as the theology in the Gospel, suggest that Matthew's Gospel was written sometime in the eighties or nineties on the borders between Palestine and Syria. It reflects not only the deep rift between Judaism and Christianity but also the struggle that was going on within the church between the remnants of Jewish Christianity, with its strict legalism, and Gentile Christianity, with its enthusiastic tendencies.

Here we already have some indication of the excitement and tension which pervade the whole Gospel. On the one hand stands the implacable enemy, Pharisaic Judaism, with its hypocrisy and rigid legalism. The Pharisees have lost sight of the true will of God, the perfect righteousness (5:20), the realization of compassion and love toward the brother—and replaced it with their own traditions and ritualistic hairsplittings. And they have rejected their promised Messiah.

On the other hand, Matthew is engaged in a deadly struggle with the enthusiasts inside the church. For this party the era of the law and the prophets had been brought to an end with the coming of Jesus (5:17 ff.). Jesus was merely the *Kyrios* ("Lord") in whose name his followers, inspired by his spirit, were able to prophesy, expel demons, and perform miracles (7:22). Against these "false prophets" (7:15 ff.) the evangelist asserts the abiding validity of the law down to the last jot and tittle. This he does by incorporating into his work a radical Jewish Christian tradition which could hardly have been formulated by Jesus himself (5:18 f.), and by announcing the final rejection of those who say "Lord, Lord," but do not do the will of God (7:21 ff.).

Despite 5:17–19, Matthew is anything but a stickler for the literal observance of the law. For Jesus authoritatively asserted the authentic will of God, which is unconditioned love, even for the enemy. And he did not merely teach it; he lived it out in his own life. He proved himself to be the promised and chosen Son of God by his unconditional obedience, not by magic arts or demonstrations of power (4:1–11).

There are many other christological titles to be found in Matthew's Gospel, such as Emmanuel, king, Son of David, Son of man, Lord, servant of God. But Matthew is not elaborating on Jewish messianic hopes. The messianic dignity of Jesus is manifested in his teaching, his deeds, his conduct, and his fate. In these the Scriptures are fulfilled in every detail. This is brought out in the tradition of Jesus' teaching, which in Matthew is greatly expanded as compared with Mark.

This didactic concern stamps the whole Gospel. Many forms of Jewish teaching which were customary in the synagogues of the contemporary diaspora are preserved in Matthew. Jesus is first and foremost a teacher. His sayings are arranged in extended discourses (actually collections of sayings) inserted into the Marcan framework: the Sermon on the Mount (5–7); the missionary charge (10); the parables of the kingdom (13); the community rule (18); the woes on the Pharisees (23); and the eschatological discourse and parables (24–25).

Similarly, the evangelist has thoroughly reshaped the miracles, making them the occasion for instruction and dialogue and pruning down the narrative detail. The same process can be seen in the shaping of the legendary material (see above, pp. 37 f.).

Just as Jesus is the one and only teacher of the church (23:8), so his followers, to whom the discourses are addressed, are consistently called disciples, meaning pupils. This is the only ecclesiological term in Matthew. Both terms, "teacher" and "disciple," express what the community has in common with Judaism and also what separates the two. For this "rabbi" is unique, unlike any other Jewish teacher or any other Christian teacher. Unlike the scribes and Pharisees, he came to "fulfill" the law and the prophets (5:17), as one "with authority" (7:29). His teaching stands in radical contrast to what was "said of old" ("But I say to you . . ."; cf. 5:21–48). Unlike the students of the rabbis and the Greek philosophers, who all eventually graduate, Jesus' disciples never stop being his pupils. Matthew's understanding of the church is steeped in this notion, as may be seen at the end of the Gospel where the risen One charges his emissaries to make "disciples" of all nations (28:19).

In Matthew we encounter for the first and only time in the Gospels the word *ecclesia* ("church," "community"). In the Greek Old Testament the ecclesia is Israel, the people of God. But in Matthew the word is filled with new meaning: "You are Peter [the "rock man"], and on this rock will I build *my* church, and the power of death [the eschatological power of evil] shall never conquer it" (16:18). The community put this word into the mouth of the earthly Jesus, a word that points to the time after Jesus' death and resurrection. This period, however, will be a continuation of earthly history, distinct from the Last Judgment and the kingdom of heaven. During this period Peter, the first disciple and spokesman of the twelve, is entrusted with teaching and disciplinary authority (in the technical language of Judaism, the power "to bind and to loose"). This authority is not attached to his person, still less to a single successor. According to Matthew 18, the same authority is given to the whole community (cf. also John 20:23).

This is not the place to discuss the extraordinary consequences this saying has had in history. What is important for the understanding of Matthew's Gospel is to note that the text speaks of "the church" in a universal sense. The church is not a local community like a Jewish synagogue, based on the law of Moses, on circumcision and other rites, and subordinated to the Temple in Jerusalem. The unifying factor in the Christian community is the presence of the Lord, to whom is given all authority in heaven and on earth to the end of time.

But in what way is he present? That is the question on which, in Matthew's church, the spirits part company. In opposition to the perfectionism and spiritual enthusiasm which does away with the barriers of time and history, the risen Lord calls the church back to the teaching of the earthly Jesus (". . . teaching them to observe all that I have commanded you," 28:20). Here is the coup de grace for any illusion the disciples might entertain that they have already reached their goal. But this does not diminish the promise of salvation in the slightest. The Beatitudes come before any of the commandments of Jesus (5:3 ff.). First priority still belongs to his work of mercy as the shepherd of the harassed flock (9:36), as the light of those in the shadow of death (4:15 f.), as the servant of God who took upon himself the sickness and suffering of men (8:17; 12:18 ff.) and called the least of men his brethren (25:31 ff.). Under his impulse, however, the disciples are called not only to hear but also to do (7:24 ff.). The prospect of judgment and the separation of the just from the unjust still hangs over the church (13:36 ff., 47 ff.). For "many are called, but few are chosen" (22:14). In Matthew every one of the discourses addressed to the disciples ends on this eschatological note.

Conditioned as he is by the traditions that have come down to him, and by his own situation, this evangelist preserves the message of Jesus and at the same time gives it a currently relevant interpretation. This should emerge clearly from the pointers we have given here.

The Savior of the World (*Luke*)

The third Gospel, attributed to the companion of Paul, is the first of a two-volume set, the other being the Acts of the Apostles. Here for the first time the earthly ministry of Jesus concludes with the ascension (Luke 24; Acts 1). The author then continues with the story of the spread of Christianity over the Roman Empire through the power of the Spirit, and ends with Paul preaching in the imperial capital (Acts 28). The provenance of Luke-Acts is unknown, but it was probably composed in the last decade of the first century.

Luke views the history of Jesus from a distance, as is shown by the time span he covers. He is also interested in the way the history of Jesus is extended in the ongoing life of the church. Both aspects, the distance and the continuity, occupy the author in a way quite foreign to the other evangelists, although their works are not far apart in date of composition.

In his own way, Luke is just as much a theologian as the other evangelists are, but he writes with a historical interest too. We have already noted the polished style of the dedication at the beginning of his Gospel, similar to the dedications in other historical works (1:1–4; cf. Acts 1:1 f.). He refers to the endeavors of his predecessors and names the witnesses who can vouch for the tradition, but he emphasizes just as strongly what he wishes to improve upon. He has "gone over" everything from the very beginning with precision and aims at reproducing it in correct order. His basic principle is unmistakable: not only back to the sources, but also back to the facts. He would have us understand his Gospel as a life of Jesus.

The only question is, How far was he successful in carrying out his intention? The truth is, his work leaves a lot to be desired. The tradition he received was such that it refused strict biographical treatment. And it is to the author's credit that he did not force his own ideas upon it. On the whole, those ideas appear only in the redactional elements; they show up in the details. For example, he places Jesus' birth (2:1 ff.) and the appearance of John the Baptist and Jesus in the wider context of world history (3:1 ff.). He alludes to the siege of Jerusalem (19:34 f.; 21:20). He regroups separate scenes and tries to make the story more intelligible psychologically. Again, he allows more space for the prelude (1–2) and portrays the sufferings of Jesus as the prototype of martyrdom.

However, Luke is far from historicizing the tradition through and through. In the main, he goes to work in the same way as the other synoptists had done. Only to a relative degree have his views on history altered the meaning and substance of the tradition and given it a shape different from that of the other evangelists. The original tradition is the primary mold of Luke's theology, just as it was with the others. This needs special emphasis today, when attempts are being made to reconstruct Luke's distinctive theology of history, justified though they are.

Despite the external and internal links which hold both parts of his work together, Luke's Gospel is so molded by the tradition that it still makes good sense for the Gospel to have been separated from the Acts and put with the other synoptics.

The evangelist had more special material at his disposal than the others, and quite valuable material too. In fact, almost half of his Gospel consists of special material. It portrays Jesus as the one who proclaimed the searching, protective love of God which refuses to give up anyone for lost. God's love is not a timeless truth, even as God is not just the eternally forgiving Father. It is something that happens, an event that is realized when Jesus turns to the publicans and sinners (5:1 ff.; 7:36 ff.; 15; 19:1 ff.; 23:34, 43) and champions the outcasts who were ostracized on nationalistic, religious, or moral grounds (for example the Samaritans, 10:29 ff.; 17:11 ff.). Luke's portrait of Christ is decisively shaped by this leitmotiv, and this is particularly true of Jesus in his majesty. Jesus is the *Kyrios,* but as such he is also the Savior of the world (2:11). Other motifs, such as the dereliction on the cross, or the picture of the Son of man who will come to judge the world, either recede into the background or vanish completely.

Jesus' story, according to Luke, belongs to the past, but it is not dead and done with. It belongs to a period of its own, a period that is quite unique. It is the "center of time" (Conzelmann). This means that Luke's historical perspective is different from that of the other synoptists. The period of the earthly Jesus lies way back in the past. Since then the church has had a history of its own. It must master these experiences in the practical tasks of faith and life. The expectation of the imminent end of the world and the return of Christ has been overlaid by other considerations. Even the other Gospels show clear signs of a delay in the Parousia. But only Luke tries to carry that experience to its logical conclusion by giving the church a new orientation in world history.

This is why he has revised the Jesus tradition. Sayings like Mark 1:15 (cf. Matt. 4:17), which speak of the kingdom of God as an imminent reality, have no parallel in Luke. In fact, there is an explicit warning against those who announce that "the time is near" (21:8 f.). Cosmic catastrophes are not "the beginning of birth pangs" as in Mark 13:7 ff.

But this does not mean that all expectation of the kingdom, the end of the world, and redemption has disappeared. Rather, it has been detached from the question of date. Only under this changed perspective has the evangelist taken up the apocalyptic sayings in the Jesus tradition (17:22 ff.; 21:25 ff.). Closely connected with this is another consideration. Warnings and instructions to persevere in faith and prayer, to maintain a humble estimate of ourselves, to be honest in our stewardship of earthly wealth and steadfast in love occupy a large amount of space in Luke's Gospel. Part of the same picture, too, is his characteristic reflection on a divine history—"salvation history"—articulated in terms of epochs and periods and embedded in the total course of secular history.

This theology, already discernible in the Gospel, becomes even more evident in the Acts of the Apostles. It is unquestionably the result of the passage of time. Nothing quite like it could have been expected in the earlier tradition about Christ as we have it in the first two evangelists.

APPENDIX: *The Acts of the Apostles*

In the second part of his historical work, also dedicated to Theophilus, Luke enters upon uncharted territory. It had not occurred to anyone before to continue the story of Jesus' deeds on earth with a description of the dissemination of the Christian message by his accredited envoys, and in this sense to write a history of the church. Nor did anyone afterward imitate what Luke had done. Thus he became the first church historian (Dibelius), but with a proviso: he is a historian in a theological sense. Luke's history is a salvation history. As in the Gospel, he is a historian and a theologian in one.

The title "Acts of the Apostles" comes from the Latin canon, which from early times called the book *Acta Apostolorum*. This title is not a very adequate description for a book which contains so much else besides. It focuses atten-

tion too much on the apostles and their deeds. Such an interest is certainly present, but it is a subordinate one. A more
important concern is the spread of the gospel and the growth
of the church. Only later, as romantic legends of miracles,
travels, and martyrdoms of particular apostles multiplied,
did an independent interest in these sainted figures develop.
In the first part of Acts the only apostle we hear about in
detail is Peter. And after his miraculous escape from prison
under Herod (12:1 ff.), he ceases to play a leading role.

The story continues without a break, dealing henceforth
with the labors of other messengers, mainly Paul and his
mission among the Gentiles. The turning point in Acts is
neither Peter's disappearance from the scene nor the first
mention of Saul/Paul (7:58), or his conversion (9),
but the lengthy account of the apostolic council (15). The
apostles in Jerusalem declare the justification and necessity
of the Gentile mission and issue clear guidelines for its exe-
cution (the "apostolic decree," 15:22 ff.; see below, pp. 88
ff.). Up to this watershed Luke's account has been focused
on Jerusalem; from there on he turns to the nations of the
world and to Rome itself.

The quantity of material about Paul shows that the author
intends his work to be a memorial to that great missionary
to the Gentiles. It is therefore all the more surprising that
Luke never calls him an apostle. There is one exception,
where the term is applied to both Barnabas and Paul (14:4,
14). Luke probably copied this from his sources, where it
carried the wider sense of "missionary." In this particular
passage the term is not as yet limited to the twelve, who
were chosen by Jesus during his earthly life and, after the
death of Judas, restored to their original number by the
election of Matthias (Acts 1:15 ff.).

This single observation points at once to the picture of the earliest church and its history which dominates the whole of Acts. Jerusalem, the scene of Jesus' death, resurrection, and ascension, and the site of the earliest community, is from the very outset a factor of major importance to the church as it spreads throughout the world. The twelve retain a leading role and control the whole movement. They guarantee the tradition, especially at the point where the gospel message is taken across the border of Judea into Samaria (8:5 ff.) and on into the Gentile world (10–11; 13–14). Only after his legitimation by the original apostles (15) at Jerusalem does Paul embark upon the worldwide mission which was his distinctive role. Even if he is not himself an apostle, he carries out the program which the risen One had laid down in his charge to the apostles (1:8).

Connected with the central role assigned to Jerusalem is another important idea characteristic of Luke's theology of history, namely the continuity between Judaism and Christianity. Christianity, hallowed by the Old Testament revelation of God and confirmed by the fulfillment of prophecy in history, is the legitimate heir of the true religion of the fathers, to which the Jews themselves had been unfaithful. Paul, as he is portrayed by Luke, declares himself a faithful Pharisee (26:2 ff.) right to the end, and seeks to win his skeptical compatriots for Jesus and the kingdom of God (28:23 ff.) by appealing to the law of Moses and the prophets. As will be seen at once, this is no longer the historical Paul who regards his origin as a member of the privileged people of God and his zeal as a Pharisee for the law as sheer loss, to be surrendered for Christ's sake (Phil. 3:5 ff.), who preaches Christ as the end of the law (Rom. 10:4), and justification by faith alone, not by works.

Luke's picture of history will not stand up to critical examination. In this and in the harmonizing tendencies of his theology he is the spokesman for the postapostolic age, when the conflicts, problems, and experiences of Paul and his contemporaries were largely forgotten. At any rate, these matters were no longer living issues. We may also assume that Luke knew nothing of Paul's letters, for he never quotes or refers to them. The collection of Pauline letters can hardly have begun before the end of the first century.

Yet Luke would have us appreciate him as a historian too, though in the ancient, not in the modern sense. Of course the materials available to him for the history of the church were very different from those he used for his Gospel. They were disparate and diffuse, and we do not know how he got hold of them. Whether he had fixed sources, and if so to what extent, is impossible to ascertain at this distance. In any case, he collected reports of varying historical worth, and commented on them to the best of his ability. These reports dealt with events, miracles, exploits, dates, travel routes, and the places, persons, and communities visited. But Luke shows himself to be a historian of his age not so much in all this detail as in the artistry with which he narrates each individual scene. The scenes are vivid and often dramatic. Evidence of this will be found in many parts of the book and is too extensive to mention here.

One feature of Luke's art as a historian which he shares with his contemporaries is to be found in the long speeches which are so typical of Acts. There are no less than twenty-four of them, covering almost a third of the entire work. They are not what Paul or anyone else actually said, they are not taken from notes or transcripts, nor are they excerpts from actual speeches. They are compositions of the author himself, inserted at high points and transitions in the story. They reflect primarily his own ideas, not those of the actual speakers. Even so, they are not unrelated to the situation, the environment, or the audience. Examples will be found in Peter's sermon at Pentecost (2:14 ff.), Stephen's speech (7:2 ff.), and Paul's speech on the Areopagus (17:22 ff.), to mention only a few.

It follows that where Luke writes as a "historian," he can hardly be considered a reliable witness to the actual events according to modern standards. Reliable information is to be sought rather in unobtrusive notices of quite incidental character, especially where these are confirmed by the authentic letters of Paul. For a long time it was thought that certain passages where the narrative switches suddenly from the third person singular to the first person plural (16:10 ff.; 20:5 ff.; 21:1 ff.; 27:1–28:16), the so-called we-sections, came from a diary written by a travel companion. But the flaw in this assumption shows up in the fact that these passages are indistinguishable in vocabulary and style from their context. In any case, such breaks in the narrative are a common device of ancient historians, their purpose being to add an air of liveliness to the story.

The historical value of Acts, after having been gauged by all these different factors, is by no means purely negative. The book of Acts remains what it has always been, a highly important source of the history of the early church and even of Paul himself. But it must always be used critically. It is primarily a source for the history of the age in which it was written, an age marked by far-reaching changes in the conditions of life and in religious opinion. The author sets before his contemporaries an idealized picture of the early church and its history as it is led forward step by step according to God's plan, at the impulse of the Holy Spirit and under the word and name of Jesus. This, Luke hopes, will provide the church with a firm foundation for its life in the world and equip it for the great assize when Jesus, who was attested by God during his earthly life (2:22) and exalted to heaven, shall return to judge at the end of time (17:31).

3. The Gospel According to Paul

The history of early Christian literature begins with letters, an utterly unliterary type of writing. The first to use—and use exclusively—this form of self-expression is the apostle Paul. There is nothing to suggest that he ever intended to write any other literary works, like the commentaries of his contemporary Philo, or theological or philosophical treatises, or a gospel like the evangelists who came after him. Paul was often imitated—though never equaled—as a letter writer; indeed, he very soon started a trend. Even after his death, the letter remained the commonest and most typical means of communication in the early church. Twenty-one of the twenty-seven books of the New Testament are letters, thirteen of them—rightly or wrongly—attributed to Paul. Even the book of Revelation is designed as a letter, or at least it begins and ends like one.

A considerable number of the New Testament letters attributed to Paul were unquestionably written, or more accurately, dictated, by him. These include the major letters to the Corinthians and Romans, as well as the shorter letters of First Thessalonians, Galatians, and Philippians, and the little Letter to Philemon. In other cases the Pauline authorship is disputed (2 Thessalonians, Colossians, and Ephesians). In a few instances the arguments against Pauline authorship are very strong (1 and 2 Timothy, Titus). The authentic epistles are without exception real letters, documents which either arose out of living communication, as is generally the case, or were intended to establish it (Romans).

In every instance Paul's letters are written by a particular author and addressed to a particular circle of readers, not to a general public. They are always conditioned by and related to a definite situation, even if other matters arise in the course of writing to overshadow it. This is what makes Paul's letters so attractive, although it also makes them more difficult for the later reader to understand. The letters are truly contemporary in character. The experiences and problems, the language, opinions, and modes of thought, both of the author and of his recipients, belong to the world in which they lived and are no longer exactly the same as our own. Many allusions and references, even direct attacks aimed at other parties, which the original readers could understand immediately and which required no explanation, need to be elucidated if they are not to remain obscure.

We should not be overly eager to bridge this historical distance. It is only too tempting to do so—witness many of the modern translations and the jargon of preachers and teachers with which we are all too familiar. What they hope to do is to make Paul and other early Christian writers relevant for the present day, but they fail to realize that in the very attempt they are actually preventing the early writers from saying what they have to say. That sort of thing pre-empts the place of the would-be hearer. More than other biblical writings, Paul's epistles refuse to be treated in such a familiar way. Yet, if we really make the effort, it will some-times surprise us how easily we can cross the barrier of many centuries and get involved in the lively dialogue between the apostle and his communities. Properly understood, the time-conditioned character of the letters does not justify us in dismissing them as no longer relevant. Rather, it points up their relevance, showing that the letters do not deal with the Christian message in a timeless vacuum. Instead, they speak directly to the experiences of daily life, to right and wrong behavior, and to the needs and aspirations of the recipients. Either explicitly or tacitly they allow the recipients as well as the author to have their own say.

Yet to dub the letters of Paul "time-conditioned writings for a specific occasion" would be no more than a provisional judgment, open to misunderstanding and quite inadequate. It would not do justice to their peculiarity and their unique position in the epistolary literature of the ancient world. One need only recall how many of our familiar categories do not fit them. They are not private letters written to a friendly group of fellow believers—possibly after necessary business has been dealt with—in order to foster personal or social relations. Nor is it their purpose to convey information like official church announcements. They are not theological treatises, sermon outlines, evangelistic tracts, or anything of that sort.

In the last resort, the letters are by their very nature and in the manner of their composition an expression and instru-ment of Paul's unique mission as an apostle. In the limited time left before the Parousia he had to carry the message of

Christ as Lord and Savior of all to the whole Gentile world. The very fact that he had to write so many letters is significant. As the evidence shows, the letters which have survived are but a small fraction of what Paul actually wrote. Their volume, already considerable, reflects the way Paul understood the gospel and his own mission. The worldwide range of his commission and the short time available ruled out any longer stay in the communities he had founded or in their vicinity. He had to be on the road again as soon as possible, leaving them to their own devices and trusting others to carry on the work he had started. To help the young and often struggling communities he frequently sent co-workers and sometimes paid them fleeting visits in person. But in the main he tried to meet their needs by his letters.

Of course the communities he writes to are only a minute group of believers surrounded and almost overwhelmed by a predominantly pagan world. They are cut adrift from the shelter of the Jewish synagogue and even persecuted by it; they are threatened from within and without. Yet for Paul each separate community was the advance guard of the whole region. These communities were located in Galatia, Macedonia, Achaia (roughly equivalent to classical Greece but having in the meantime become a Roman province), Asia (the district covering the coastal cities of Asia Minor), and finally Rome itself, which was not only the capital of the empire but also a bridgehead to other regions further west (Spain; see below, pp. 105 ff.).

Yet it would be quite wrong to imagine the apostle dashing ahead in all directions and preaching the gospel without a plan, fired by apocalyptic fantasy or an unbalanced temperament, like some kind of roving reporter. His letters show the close relationship which had grown up even in a short time between the apostle and his communities, a relationship involving trust and love as well as mistrust, tension, and sometimes even alienation.

It is amazing how Paul overcomes the barriers of time and space, wearing himself out unceasingly in body and spirit, caring for communities and even for individual converts. He is familiar with their specific circumstances, their strengths and their weaknesses, and he always keeps abreast of what is going on. All of this comes out abundantly in his letters. But he relates everything to the Christ event. All his communities are drawn into this event through the word he has proclaimed. They all have a part in it, even the Galatians when they are on the verge of apostasy and the Corinthians when they have nearly succumbed to enthusiasts and false teachers. In the midst of all this confusion Paul still believes they are called by God and belong to Christ.

With one exception all of the genuine Pauline letters are addressed to communities, to be read aloud when the people assembled for worship. Paul wrote them in his capacity as an apostle called by God and a slave of Jesus Christ. Even the little Letter to Philemon, despite its personal tone, is not a normal kind of private letter. It is addressed to one of the apostle's fellow workers and to the church in his house. A slave of Philemon had apparently stolen money from his master and run away. In due course he sought refuge with the apostle, who at the time was probably in prison at Ephesus. In his letter, Paul straightens out the wretched affair. Significantly, however, he writes even here as "the prisoner of Jesus Christ," appealing to his position as father in God to the "ne'er-do-well" (a play on the slave's name, Onesimus, which means "the useful one"). For in the meantime the runaway slave had been converted, and Paul asks his master to receive him back, no longer as a slave but as a brother. From now on Philemon himself must be an "Onesimus" to Paul. The letter to Philemon is an instructive contribution to the much-discussed subject of slavery in early Christianity.

In regard to style the Pauline letters incorporate—notably in the opening and conclusion—the convention of classical and especially Jewish and oriental letter writing of naming the writer and recipients, and expressing greetings and good wishes. But there is something distinctive about Paul's letters. In introducing himself he includes his colleagues as fellow writers. He has a special word for the recipients, and turns the conventional greeting into a Christian blessing. These features make his letters quite different from other epistolary literature of classical antiquity, as mentioned above. Paul's letters also depart from convention by including a good deal of doctrinal teaching, exposition of Scripture (e.g., Rom. 4; 1 Cor. 10:1 ff.; Gal. 3–4), extensive theological argumentation (Rom. 9–11), and concise summaries of the gospel message couched in stereotyped formulas or modeled on such formulas (Rom. 1:3 f.; 1 Cor. 15:3 ff.). Elsewhere there are apocalyptic fragments in traditional style (1 Cor. 15:20 ff., 51 ff.; 1 Thess. 4:15 ff.), as well as stylized ethical exhortation (paraenesis) without specific reference to any concrete situation (catalogues of virtues and vices and household codes).

As instruments and documents of his apostolic ministry Paul's letters are a genuine early Christian literary creation. They are the counterpart of that other genre, the gospels, which of course are later than Paul (see above, pp. 30, 41).

The strong influence Paul had on his successors is shown by many other early Christian writings, both canonical and extracanonical. This is still true despite the fact that the Pauline letters were hardly in general circulation during his lifetime or even immediately after his death. As we have seen, the process of publication did not begin to any great extent until several decades later. The exchange of this and other elements of tradition between the various communities was much more gradual, more haphazard, and more sporadic than we are inclined to think.

Many of the New Testament "letters" which are in epistolary form have the content characteristic of a different literary genre. There are church orders (the Pastorals), homilies or sermons (Hebrews), collections of ethical sayings (James), and polemical or didactic apocalyptic writings (Jude, 2 Peter). True, the border line between one genre and another is often a fluid one. As a literary form the letter was already favored in classical antiquity (we have, for example, letters of philosophers and of Horace); and there are occasional examples of it in modern literature (Goethe's *Werther,* for instance).

The genuine letters of Paul are easily distinguished from artificial letters by the fact that they are just that, real letters. They make sense only if they are read in the context of Paul's life and the life of his communities. So it is advisable to discuss them here under this aspect rather than in the order in which they appear in the New Testament. Only in this way do they acquire real point and begin to speak to us. They cease to be a mere reservoir of liturgical lessons or devotional readings, as long tradition has inured us to accept them. To regard them in this traditional way is a pity, and the consequences of it are widely known. For the modern reader of the Bible Paul has become, like so many other early Christian writers, a saint in a stained-glass window, so

devoid of flesh and blood and so lacking in individual characteristics that they are really interchangeable. We tend to
picture these men as they appear in early Christian or medi-
eval art, where what they look like is largely a matter of
accident and each has acquired certain legendary attributes or
conventional designations that set him apart from the others.

THE LIFE AND TEACHING OF PAUL

We must now try to relate Paul's letters to his life and
work. This does not mean subscribing to the popular but
erroneous notion that his letters are from start to finish a
record of his subjective experience, reflective of his gifts as a
visionary or as an eager Jew constantly frustrated in his
quest for moral and religious perfection. Paul's background,
tradition, social milieu and education, his gifts and talents,
are obvious enough. So, too, are the uniqueness and richness
of his character and the sudden outbursts of temper which
occur so frequently in his letters. Yet the key to his letters
is not to be found in his self-understanding. So to construe
them would be to do violence to the texts themselves. On the
whole it is only rarely, albeit at important junctures, that his
own person and life's history come to the surface, and then
only when they have something to contribute to the understanding of Christ and the cosmic dimensions of his saving
work.

All the same, Paul's life and work are of great importance
for the understanding of his letters. All the letters, without
exception, were composed toward the end of his career and
within a relatively short span of time. They cover a period of
no more than six or seven years when he worked as a missionary before being taken prisoner on his last visit to
Jerusalem (ca. A.D. 56–57), after which he probably died a

martyr's death in Rome in the early sixties, during the reign of Nero. To understand Paul's letters, however, it is necessary to go back to the period immediately after his conversion and apostolic call, a period roughly three times as long.

Neither the letters nor Acts give us any exact dates. But there is a reference to the proconsulship of Gallio in Acts 18:12, a date which is fixed by an inscription (probably between A.D. 51 and 52). From this we can place Paul's first stay of eighteen months in Corinth between the end of A.D. 49 and the early summer of 51. Then from this point and with the help of other scattered references we can work out a chronology for the life of Paul and the history of early Christianity with some degree of accuracy.

Paul never wrote with an autobiographical end in view, and as a result we can reconstruct only a fragmentary outline of his life. Nevertheless, the letters are highly informative in this respect. And in any case, they are the best and most authentic source we have for gauging all the other extant information about him.

As we have already seen, this also holds good for the Acts of the Apostles and the traditions incorporated in that book. The existence of such traditions shows that after Paul had finished his labors certain communities treasured a good deal of detailed information about his life. There were remarkable stories about the exploits and miracles of the great man. Much of it was patterned on the stories of divine men that were then current in the surrounding pagan world. Luke devoted considerable space to these traditions, and there are further examples of the same type in the later apocryphal Acts of Paul, where they really run riot. Luke developed such stories further in his own way in line with his postapostolic view of history. Yet when submitted to critical scrutiny these traditions yield much plausible information about the life of Paul.

Born probably around the turn of the century at Tarsus in Cilicia, the son of a Jewish family in the Hellenistic diaspora (Acts 22:3), Paul was not only faithful to his ancestral heritage but became a strict Pharisee. He remained so until after the death of Jesus and the beginnings of the Christian community in Jerusalem and in the Hellenistic world (Phil. 3:5 ff.; Gal. 1:13 f.). Carrying his Pharisaism to its logical conclusion, he persecuted the followers of Jesus, as he repeatedly tells us (Gal. 1:23; Phil. 3:6; 1 Cor. 15:9; cf. Acts 9:1 ff.; 22:4 f.; 26:9 ff.), though the circumstances were not exactly as Luke pictured them later. Luke credits the high priests with a jurisdiction extending to the synagogues outside of Judea (Damascus), which they never had to that extent. The real situation was somewhat different. Christians were sentenced to flogging and expelled from the synagogue, the same sort of thing Paul himself often had to suffer later (2 Cor. 11:24).

Why did he throw himself into the persecution of Christians with such zeal? He gives us a clear explanation in passages like Gal. 1:13 ff. and Phil. 3:5 f., where he refers to his activities as a persecutor in connection with his zeal for the law. He thought the adherents of Jesus, like their Master himself, were out to destroy the law. True, Paul could hardly have regarded all the Christians who remained in Jerusalem as enemies of the law and blasphemers against God. Under the leadership of the original apostles this group remained faithful to the holy city, the Temple, and the law. In that regard there can be no doubt that Acts is right. The Jerusalem Christians had no thought of breaking away from the people of God and cutting themselves off from its privileges.

At first the only thing that distinguished them from other Jews was their belief that after his death on the cross Jesus had risen again and would soon return as Messiah. That, for the Jews, was at worst a strange illusion, certainly no cause for bringing Christians to court or expelling them from the community. That sort of apocalyptic enthusiasm would crop up again later. It became an intolerable threat to the foundation of the Jewish religion and a major internal crisis for the Christian community only after the growth of radical Hellenistic-Jewish tendencies under the leadership of Stephen (Acts 6–7), which of course came quite soon. This party questioned the exclusive claims of the Jewish people to salvation and by doing so triggered off the first Christian persecution. One of its incidental consequences was the establishment of the first Gentile Christian community in Syria (Damascus and Antioch). The exact course of events, so crucial for the history of early Christianity and for Paul himself, can only be read between the lines in Acts (8–9; 11:19 ff.). All that Luke could do was to put together a quite inadequate account which sought to harmonize the conflicting tendencies in the early church.

There is one fact given by Luke on which both Paul and Luke agree: Paul's persecution was directed against the Christians in Damascus, and it was either in Damascus or thereabouts that the turning point of his life and his call to be apostle to the Gentiles occurred.

What exactly prepared the way for this call? Where did Paul first come face-to-face with the Christian message and under what circumstances? What obstacles had he first to overcome? On all of these questions the sources are silent, however much we should like to satisfy our curiosity. These questions are not only unanswerable but, compared with the cause which lay closest to the apostle's heart, also unimportant. All we can say with certainty is that his conversion and calling were not occasioned by the direct impact of Jesus' preaching during his earthly ministry; Paul never met Jesus (2 Cor. 5:16). But neither did his conversion happen gradually. It is not the case that Paul came to realize more and more the futility of his attempts to keep the law until in the end he suffered a spiritual crisis. This view has been widely held, but it is based on a misleading interpretation of Rom. 7:7–25 as an autobiographical account. In this passage Paul is not telling the story of his own wasted life. He is speaking of mankind as a whole, its lost state and its bondage to sin, the law, and death, viewed in the light of the Christ event.

As a matter of fact, the sudden appearance of the risen and ascended Lord at Damascus brought home to Paul not the error and inferiority of the law but the greatness of the grace of God. God's grace was not just an intervention in Paul's personal life but a liberation of cosmic dimensions (Gal. 1:15 f.). To pass this message along to the Gentiles was from now on his mission and the theme of his theology. He summarizes it in his teaching about the righteousness of God which is revealed apart from the works of the law, through Christ alone and by faith alone (Rom. 3:21 ff.).

Formulated as it is in a strange Jewish language and worn thin by long Christian usage, the doctrine of justification is not easily intelligible in our day. For modern man the primary question overshadowing all others is whether there is a God at all. Justification seems stale, out of date, no longer "with it." It seems tied to a view of the world which we no longer share. True, Paul never discusses the existence of God, but he would repudiate the suggestion that it is a question of world view. Paul's teaching about the law and justification by faith alone transcends the kind of questions raised by modern man and the way he thinks. For Paul, you can talk about God only if at the same time you talk about the world and man. The converse is equally true: you cannot talk about man or the world without raising the question about God. The whole of Paul's thinking moves within these poles — God's search for man and man's search for God.

But Paul never indulges in timeless abstractions. His thought always has reference to Jesus Christ and to the effect of his life upon the world, this Jesus whose life by all human standards ended in the tragedy of the cross (1 Cor. 1:18 ff.). Paul's gospel is the "word of the cross." Its burden is the "righteousness of God." As he says, it was not this Jesus, not God, not even the law that came to a tragic end, but man, be he Jew or Gentile, devout or superstitious — all men who, whether consciously or unconsciously, try to domesticate God in their own lives.

This urge for self-vindication and self-assertion, this desire to wrest an absolute meaning from life by dint of personal achievement, can take various forms. But, however hidden, it is always the driving force in every life. That is how man tries to establish credit and secure recognition for himself. Take for instance the zeal of the Jew who seeks to fulfill the law of God by his own "works." The revelation of God's righteousness put an end to this quest. God is man's judge. God still has the last word. The picture of justice sitting blindfold, disregarding man's person and weighing only his deeds, is inapplicable. God never takes his eyes off man. What he does is to put man in the right and accord him recognition. God accepts man unreservedly, despite his hostility. That is the meaning of the Christ event.

For Paul faith means appropriating God's acceptance of man with an acceptance of God's grace which is just as absolute and unqualified. To believe is to know oneself accepted.

Man's fall turned out to be his salvation and his release. He was "ransomed" (Gal. 4:5) from bondage to the principalities and powers which held him under their thrall.

Men thought they had brought this Christ to his end, whereas what actually happened was that the law came to an end as a means to salvation (Rom. 10:4). For although the law was intended to give man life (Rom. 7:10), its real effect is to expose man for what he is, a creature who does everything he can to escape from his Creator. In the fond belief that he is independent and free, man succumbs to the curse of death. As Paul sees it, it was only the gospel that brought all this to light. Man owes his life to God and ought to be thankful for it. But instead man becomes a slave to himself and the world and incurs a lasting debt of guilt. Man is incapable of deciding for God, but God has decided for man and freed him through Christ for a new life in the world (Gal. 5:1, 11).

The death of Christ and his exaltation as Lord of the universe means the annulment of this curse (Gal. 3:13). By an extreme paradox Paul can speak of the "justification of the ungodly" (Rom. 4:5).

The three dramatic accounts of Paul's conversion in Acts (9:1 ff.; 22:3 ff.; 26:9 ff.), with their vivid though secondary details, tend to mislead us into supposing that Paul's vision of Christ at Damascus was the dominant theme of his missionary preaching. True, this vision is an inseparable part of the turning point of Paul's life (1 Cor. 9:1; 15:8) and his apostolic call. But Paul never makes it the subject of his preaching or his theology. He had other visions too (2 Cor.

12:1 ff.), but he is reluctant to talk about them and explicitly denies that they play any important part in his preaching. He also draws a distinction between these visions and the Easter appearance of Christ. When he does speak of that appearance, he includes himself with the other apostles who are witnesses of the resurrection, and who as such confirm the truth of the Christian message. But the decisive and unique feature of this message, which is summed up in Paul's doctrine of justification, is the universality of Christ's redeeming work. This particular version of the message was certainly not shared by the earliest community or the original apostles in Jerusalem.

In the course of his mission and in his letters the apostle to the Gentiles developed his distinctive understanding of the Christian message in many different ways. Often the presentation depends upon the kind of people who made up his communities or the stage they had reached in the faith. Thus his epistles offer a broad spectrum of theological thought which refuses to be fitted into a neat and tidy system. Yet his doctrine of justification, whether visible or not, is always the nerve center of his message. And what is more, it did not become so only after his heated controversy with the Judaizers, as has been erroneously alleged, although these later conflicts undoubtedly did contribute to the development of his teaching. Without any doubt, the doctrine of justification determined his course and his missionary activity from the very moment of his call.

Only thus can we explain the curious circumstance, completely suppressed in Acts but evidenced in Gal. 1:12 ff., that Paul did not go up to Jerusalem after his conversion in order to receive detailed instruction from the original apostles. Instead, he went straight to the Gentiles and preached the gospel of salvation to them. His first objective was Arabia, i.e., the Hellenistic kingdom of Nabatea (roughly equivalent to modern Jordan). He did not, as is often thought, retreat to the desert for silent meditation, but went there to begin his mission. It occupied him for several years and apparently was not very successful, for it ended with his persecution (2 Cor. 11:32 f.). There is not a single trace of this period in Acts. In fact, Paul was careful to stay away from Jerusalem for several more years, about fifteen all told, continuing his missionary work in Gentile Syria and Cilicia and ending up in Antioch. During this lengthy period there is only a brief interlude of two weeks spent in visiting Peter (Cephas). It is noticeable how Paul avoided contact with the leaders in Jerusalem. Apparently the reason he kept his distance was that he could not hope for much sympathy from them for his gospel of freedom from the law and openness toward the Gentiles. If this was not the reason, then one would naturally have to suspect him of obstinately insisting on his own private revelation at Damascus, and of pursuing his own missionary work for fifteen years or so in complete disregard of the Jesus tradition as it was preserved by the original apostles. It is hard to imagine a worse misinterpretation or one more contrary to Paul's intentions.

Paul certainly attached great importance to the original Jerusalem community and to the unity of Jews and Gentiles in a single church. There is nothing to suggest that he ever intended to found isolated coteries like those of the mystery religions. This is evidenced by the apostolic conference in Jerusalem (ca. A.D. 48), according to the detailed accounts in Gal. 2:1–10 and Acts 15 probably the most important event in the history of early Christianity. The question at issue was whether Paul's gospel of freedom from the law was to have full recognition and whether the Gentiles could become full members of the church without first joining the Jewish people of God by being circumcised as the Old Testament required. After a fierce struggle, of which not a hint has survived in Acts 15, Paul extracted from the original apostles an unconditional agreement, including the acceptance of the Gentile Christian communities. It was not just a weak compromise. There was no question of making the Jerusalem church accept "Paulinism," or of doubting their missionary responsibility toward the Jews.

One of the chief results of the apostolic conference, according to Paul, was the decision made in the opposite direction. The original Jewish community, with its very different outlook, was given full recognition by the Gentile Christian community as represented by Barnabas and Paul. This meant the unity of Christ's church, transcending all existing differences. According to Gal. 2:10 the concordat was to be sealed by a collection from the Gentile Christians for the poor of Jerusalem. The collection would become Paul's major concern in his later missionary communities, and he would devote the utmost care and energy to it. In due course it would acquire a symbolic meaning for him and determine his ultimate fate (see below, pp. 110 f.).

The later account by Luke (Acts 15) is correct in seeing the Jerusalem conference as an event of major importance in the history of the church. Unfortunately its description of the negotiations and its assessment of the outcome are quite worthless. The controversy between the two sides is not discussed. The question of circumcision is regarded as having been settled long before, and having been brought up later only quite gratuitously by an obstinate group of Pharisees. Peter — in Acts it was he who inaugurated the Gentile mission! — and James side with Barnabas and Paul right from the start and make good "Pauline" speeches in the popular sense of the term. In Luke's historical perspective it is Peter and James who carry the day (see above, pp. 67 f.).

In Acts the council culminates in a decree which lays down certain restrictions for the Gentile mission, the so-called apostolic decree (15:19 ff., 23 ff.). The Gentile converts must keep a minimum of Jewish ritual regulations. This is the exact opposite of Paul's own account (they "gave me no further instructions," Gal. 2:6, NEB marginal note), and of the practice he followed later. It is obvious that the outcome in Acts is a later, relatively liberal ruling emanating from Jewish Christian communities, a ruling of which the real Paul knew nothing. According to an account of his own, one whose authenticity is beyond all doubt, the result of the conference was that Paul was left an entirely free hand to preach salvation to the Gentiles.

These historical data and facts are not merely milestones marking the external course of Paul's life, they are actually faith become the stuff of history. One indication of this is the worldwide mission Paul planned, probably as a result of the apostolic conference. First he embarked upon the so-called second missionary journey. At least that is what Acts says, but the narrative is full of gaps, and according to the letters there were considerably more than three journeys. In any case, from this time on or, to be exact, since his first stay in Galatia, Paul began to set his sights on Rome and the western empire as the goal of his work. In favor of this is the fact that he took the direct route through Asia Minor (Acts 16:8, 10), passed through Philippi and Macedonia, and from there traveled along the Via Egnatia, the road from Rome to the east. This imperial road from Philippi via Thessalonica to Illyria (Rom. 15:19) continued on the other side of the Adriatic from Brindisi to Rome as the famous Via Appia.

Paul probably stayed longer in the communities which he founded en route by his preaching than the description of Acts would seem to imply. But he never lost sight of his ambitious plans (Rom. 1:13 ff.; 15:22 f.), although he was sidetracked by persecutions in Thessalonica. He also had to make a detour in the interior of Greece. So it was several years before he could resume his intention of going to Rome (see below, pp. 108 ff.).

Here, too, Paul's biography is a reflection of his faith and his understanding of the gospel. Here we see his faith in Christ as Lord and Savior of all, his expectation of the imminent Parousia, and his confidence that once the gospel was proclaimed and a community had been formed it would become a center for further advance. Then whole areas would be brought under the lordship of Christ, areas extending far beyond the limits of the local communities.

THE LETTERS OF PAUL

Paul's most important missionary activity in the eastern and Greek-speaking half of the empire took place within five years of his hurried departure from Thessalonica, the modern Salonica. Possibly this activity was by force of circumstances which ran counter to his original plans (see above, p. 90), but anyhow he made the best use of his time. It was during this period that all of the genuine letters were written. They vary considerably in character and show how much the apostle adapted his preaching to the needs of the communities, making it relevant and developing his thought in many different directions.

First Thessalonians

The earliest letter — the oldest written document in the New Testament — is First Thessalonians, written soon after Paul arrived at Corinth in the spring of 50. The promising beginnings of this Gentile Christian community are still quite recent and the apostle recalls them with gratitude (1:2–2:14). So too are the beginnings of Gentile hostility which forced him to flee. The same thing had happened previously at Philippi (2:2; cf. Acts 17:5 ff.). That is why he sent his companions back from Athens to encourage the Thessalonians. Meanwhile, however, he had received good news from his companions on their return to Corinth, and had also heard of problems in the community. Several of the converts had died and this raised a question. Would those who had fallen asleep before the Parousia be excluded from the final salvation? The very fact that such a question was raised shows how realistically the apostle must have spoken of the imminence of Christ's return. The idea that any who died would rise again had never occurred to his hearers. Thus Paul is obliged to deal with this question for the first time. His reply is remarkable for its bizarre apocalyptic picture of the end of the world and the Parousia. But its sole purpose is to draw out the consequences of Christ's resurrection. Neither those who have fallen asleep in faith nor the survivors will be lost. Resurrected or transformed, they will together "meet" the Lord as he comes from heaven (4:13 ff.). It makes no difference whether they are alive or dead. What then of the time and hour of the Parousia? That question is unanswerable and loses all importance. The only thing that matters is that the faithful should live as children "of the day" and "of light," "whether we are awake or asleep" (i.e., whether we are alive or dead), in the sure hope that we will always be with the Lord (5:1 ff.). In First Corinthians Paul expands these thoughts doctrinally. Strictly speaking, his earlier letter to the Thessalonians is in no way a doctrinal letter, nor does it contain any explicit echoes of his doctrine of justification. What he says is determined by the need to confirm the community in its original rejection of heathen idols to serve the true and living God and to await the salvation that has been made known through Jesus (1:10; 4:11 ff.; 5:9).

Second Thessalonians

Many scholars today ascribe the Second Letter to the Thessalonians to a later author rather than to Paul himself, and rightly so, for much of it is actually too "Pauline." It is modeled on the first letter, a practice quite contrary to Paul's usual custom. Even the wording and minute turns of phrase are identical. In fact, the second letter presupposes the literary use of the first letter. But its purpose is quite different. It is written in opposition to the doctrine of an imminent Parousia, a doctrine which it condemns as enthusiastic and heretical, involving a mistaken appeal to the apostle and to letters purporting to be from him. Much of Second Thessalonians is taken up with a long series of apocalyptic events, all happening on schedule before Christ's return for the Last Judgment (2:1 ff.). All this is quite unlike anything in the undisputed Pauline letters. Thus the close mutual relationship of the two letters, coupled with their differences, supports the contention that a later imitator composed the second letter and buttressed it by claiming Paul's apostolic authority.

First Corinthians

The next letters to be written came several years after the founding of the community in Corinth and Paul's departure from that city. All of them were probably written during his two or three years' stay at Ephesus (Acts 19:8 ff.; 20:31) about A.D. 53–55. Among these the most important is his lively correspondence with the Corinthians, which extended over a considerable period of time. This extensive correspondence is certainly not complete in the two canonical letters to the Corinthians, which were probably compiled from the large body of correspondence by a later collector. The second letter is certainly a composite, and the first letter may be also. Paul himself says he had already written a previous letter (1 Cor. 5:9). Some think certain sections from this earlier document were later incorporated into our Second Corinthians, but this is disputed. Also 2 Cor. 2:4 ff. and 7:8 speak of an intermediate letter, written in deep anxiety and concern.

The most important part of this "tearful letter" is probably preserved in 2 Corinthians 10–13, though out of chronological order. These chapters could hardly have belonged there originally, for they suddenly plunge into the middle of a highly emotional argument. The Corinthians have been led astray by false teachers into rebellion and apostasy, while in chapters 1, 2, and 7 Paul speaks movingly of the solution of this painful conflict. The seams and abrupt transitions in this letter clearly suggest different situations, not merely changes of mood and temper on the part of the apostle. Once our attention has been drawn to them, closer inspection will show that even the first nine chapters contain considerable fragments of other letters. They were obviously arranged in their present order when they were compiled into a larger work of apostolic teaching for a wider audience.

More than any other document in the New Testament, the letters to the Corinthians give us abundant insight into the growth of the Pauline missionary communities and the dangers that threatened their existence. In particular, they provide information about the period after the apostle's departure from Corinth, a period on which Luke is silent. Paul's picture of this community is anything but rosy, despite its promising development in so many directions. Its very wealth became a threat to its existence.

As early as First Corinthians we hear of divisions and conflicts within the community (1–4). There are problems of behavior (5–6) and excessive misuse of Christian freedom and Christian faith (8–10). These troubles were reflected in the community's assemblies for worship (11–14).

How does Paul deal with these various symptoms? With the utmost care and concern, but without a trace of legalism or casuistry. Although he hits hard, he never restores order simply by issuing peremptory commands. Nor does he confront heresy by reciting dogmatic propositions. Instead, he takes up each problem in turn and discusses point by point the information he has received through envoys from Corinth or by other means. He goes to the heart of the matter every time, pointing out what really counts and what cannot be given up. In this way he leads them back to faith and to a life molded by faith and lived out in fellowship. Although the variety of questions discussed is at first sight bewildering, the First Letter to the Corinthians has a unity of theme which goes far beyond the immediate occasion of its composition.

This is shown in the opening chapter by the way Paul treats the Corinthian parties. Each of the parties appeals to a great Christian leader: Paul, Apollos, Cephas, and even Christ himself (1:12). Without discussing what lies behind these slogans, Paul goes straight to the point and brings out what is wrong with all of these rival parties, his own included. They are destroying the unity of the body of Christ and denying the cross. Whatever line they take theologically, each group is motivated by an urge for self-assertion and self-expression. They want to show off their "wisdom," whereas God has made such wisdom foolishness through the "word of the cross," a scandal for the Jews and folly for the Greeks. God's no to the wisdom and conceits of man sounds harsh and brutal. But it expresses first and last the saving will of God, who will not leave the world to perish in its selfish and fallen state. It also establishes the criteria by which to judge the work of the community. Through Christ all things belong to them and they are free (3:21 ff.). As men who have thus been set free, however, they belong to Christ, they are his. For Paul this freedom is not a general truth about human nature. Man cannot realize it for himself through his own intelligence or wisdom, as the Stoics of the day believed. Rather, it is a miracle—new life through the forgiveness and grace of God. The faithful may still have to live in the world but they are not of it (6:11, 19 f.).

Paul can use the very words of such pagan philosophers as Epictetus or Seneca, as though his ideal were that of the true sage who refuses to let himself be ruled by the circumstances of life or his own desires and who stays on top when everything goes wrong. But Paul's motivation is entirely different, and so is his concept of freedom. The Stoic sage thinks he is free so long as he does not allow other people to dominate him but remains secure and self-reliant. For Paul man is not free so long as he tries to manage his own life and will not accept Christ as his Lord. Again, the apostle does not regard freedom merely as an ideal possibility. It is a reality of grace, identical with the salvation which comes from Christ. It is something man lives by. He does not have to acquire it, it is something he must maintain and prove. He does this by exercising self-control in the face of sexual desire (5:1 ff.; 6:12 ff.), and by renouncing his own rights (6:1 ff.)—whether in married life or in his religious and social relationships (7:1 ff., 17 ff.)—as he awaits the imminent coming of the Lord (7:29 ff.).

The Corinthian enthusiasts did not regard themselves as Stoic sages any more than Paul. They were Christians who based their freedom on their religion. They considered themselves superior not only to the world but also to their less sophisticated Christian brethren. They knew they were already perfect and enjoyed a profound knowledge of revelation. They were filled with the Spirit of God and thought they had a right to flaunt their freedom before others, regardless of their feelings. In this "gnostic" manner they confronted Paul (8:1) with slogans which he could not simply reject (2:6 ff.; 8–10), though he understood them in a radically different sense. "I am free to do anything" (6:12; 10:23)—Paul might have said that, too. But for the Corinthians this meant, "Nothing can touch my true, divine ego." This "freedom" they practiced accordingly with equal thoughtlessness, especially in their sexual, cultic, and social behavior, without concern for the weaker brethren. For Paul, on the other hand, there is only one test for Christian freedom: Does it serve the neighbor and strengthen the community? Freedom is not just a question of one's rights. The power and authority of freedom is shown by refusing to make use of it when the life and salvation of others are at stake (8–10).

The chaos created by the Corinthians' conception of freedom was manifested chiefly in their turbulent services of worship, whose attendant disorders Paul castigates in chapters 11–14. Here he gives highly concrete, critical, and positive injunctions for the celebration of the Lord's Supper (11:19 ff.). The community with its many different gifts and the mutual coordination of its members is the one body of Christ (12). So Paul speaks of the gifts of the Spirit at work in the community (14) and of love, the greatest gift of all (13). All of these injunctions have one thing in common. Paul is never shocked by all the manifestations of the Spirit. He never tries to quench them or reduce them to a tolerable level of mediocrity. Instead, he firmly directs the welter of spiritual experience along the channels of responsibility for the neighbor.

Then follows chapter 15. This great chapter on the resurrection of the dead, which the Corinthians denied, must be understood in the same light. Though Paul's arguments may sometimes sound strange and typical of his age, their general tenor is clear. Where the Corinthian enthusiasts ignore the limitations of earthly and historical existence, and flaunt the perfection which as Christians they have already attained, Paul reminds them of the not-yet of their life in time and inspires them with hope for the future of God.

From early days and for a long time afterward primitive Christianity had to contend with gnosis, so-called. Paul's letters to the Corinthians are the earliest sign of this. But many other New Testament writings (the Fourth Gospel, the First Letter of John, the Pastorals, the Catholic Epistles, and Hebrews), to say nothing of later literature in the ancient church, bear traces of the controversy with gnosis, a dangerous foe which was destined to become the heresy par excellence. There were many different types of gnosis; it was a characteristic phenomenon of religious syncretism in the era of oriental-Hellenistic culture. It is a reflection of the decay of the old religions of the city-state since classical times and the resultant failure of nerve, the individual's fear of life and his yearning for a world beyond this one.

Gnosis was not a religion unto itself with a uniform doctrine or a separate cultic community. It was rather a tendency affecting many religions, not only ancient ones but particularly new ones, some Gentile and others Jewish or Christian in character. But wherever gnostic tendencies are at work, the effect is always the same. It involves a reinterpretation and reassessment of the revelations, doctrines, and rites of the respective religion, with the aim of satisfying the longing for redemption which was shared by all who were captivated by the gnostic movement.

Although gnosis may take different forms, it always has certain common characteristics. One of them is radical dualism. The world is the sphere of corruption, ruled by the powers of darkness. In this world the "gnostic" regards himself as an alien. His tragedy is that he has been banished from the celestial world of light and condemned to wander adrift in the world. But through "revelation" he has been reminded of his divine origin, and having acquired "knowledge" (gnosis) of his true self, he has been removed from this wicked world and made a partaker of heavenly nature in the world beyond. Which of the various gnostic notions, myths, and speculations had found their way into the Corinthian community in Paul's time we can no longer say with certainty, nor does it matter. Tendencies of this nature can be recognized at Corinth even if they are not yet developed in a speculative way. There was the "wisdom" and "knowledge" which Paul's opponents claimed, their contempt for the message of the cross, their spiritual enthusiasm, their intoxication with freedom and perfectionism, and their consciousness that they were the elite, compared with the immature brethren of the community. All of this Paul resolutely opposes, measuring the enthusiasm of the "Spirit" against the cross of Christ. He will not allow his opponents to despise the creation of God. He insists that responsibility for others is more important than personal freedom. Thus he recalls the enthusiasts to the earthly and temporal realities of human life.

Second Corinthians

The fragments collected in the so-called Second Letter to the Corinthians belong to a somewhat later period. In the meantime a new development had occurred. Wandering apostles and false spirits had penetrated the community, which was insecure enough already, and incited it to rebel against Paul and his gospel (see above, p. 94). The various layers of material that make up the "letter" can still be distinguished, at least to some extent. The canonical order gives the impression of a continuous document. If, however, the different layers are rearranged, we get a clear impression of the conflict as it develops from phase to phase. First we see it gradually warming up. Then it comes to a head, and finally, through the passionate efforts of the apostle and his fellow workers, there is a complete reconciliation.

Although the partition theory is still disputed, I personally find it convincing. According to its proposed rearrangement, the section 2:14–7:4 should be placed where it really belongs on both chronological and logical grounds, namely at the beginning. Like First Corinthians (16:8), which was presumably written from Ephesus, this fragment shows that Paul had already heard of the recent irregularities at Corinth and had a pretty clear picture of the wiles by which the intruders had seduced the community and incited its members against himself. These false teachers regarded Christ as a kind of divine power in competition with other contemporary deities. They themselves were his emissaries, whose task it was to demonstrate Christ's divinity and miraculous power by "signs and wonders."

There can be no question that this portrait of Christ and the apostles, indebted as it is to pagan models, exercised a good deal of influence on the early Hellenistic traditions about Jesus and the Christian mission, at least in its more popular forms. There are clear traces of this influence in the Gospels (see above, pp. 44 ff.), even more traces in Acts, and in the later apocryphal literature it reaches its zenith. Paul's gospel, his own appearance and activity, were diametrically opposed to this tendency. The new "apostles" seemed to sense this at once, hence the aspersions they cast on the legitimacy and authority of his apostleship. This also explains why Paul had to defend himself, in the section we have just identified, against this perversion of the gospel. The intruders had brought letters of recommendation from elsewhere, and Paul particularly condemns them for "peddling" the Christian message by accepting payment for the miracles they displayed (2:17). Despite the vigor of his polemic, the tone of the letter suggests that he is still confident that the community will side with him.

Just how close the subversive activities of his opponents had gotten to the roots is shown by Paul's sudden visit to

Corinth. There was a tremendous showdown and Paul had to leave as quickly as he had come (2:5; 7:12). Then came the "tearful letter," written from Ephesus (2:4; 7:8). Chapters 10–13, which form part of this letter, show how isolated Paul was during this conflict. But this does not trouble him. He pulls out all the stops—now imploring them, now speaking as a fool in irony. For the moment it almost looked as if the apostle were fighting a lost cause. But this letter, and the personal intervention of Titus, whom Paul sent off at the same time, were not without their effect. Paul traveled from Ephesus to Macedonia to meet Titus, longing to hear what had happened. Titus met up with him and brought the happy news that the Corinthians had seen the light. They could not do enough to show their affection for the apostle, whom they had previously scorned (the letter of reconciliation, 1:1–2:13; 7:5 ff.; written ca. 55 from Macedonia). By the time Acts was written the whole story had been forgotten.

This moving drama, however, had been much more than a very human display of personal rivalry with all of its unpleasant accompaniments—defamation of character on the one hand and insulted ambition on the other—an episode that would be of little concern for us today. More than once, in fact, Paul put his own person completely in the shade (cf. Phil. 1:12 ff.). Nor did he regard the dignity of his office as a subject that was off limits. This time, however, more than his apostleship was at stake. It was the very gospel itself. When his opponents attacked his legitimacy and his preaching, what they were really attacking was the heart of the matter, the crucified and risen Lord himself. It was a question of salvation or perdition in the ultimate sense of the word (2:15 ff.). In the language of 5:17 ff., it was an attack upon God's act of reconciliation in Christ.

Paul did not regard the gospel as a theological doctrine that could be variously expressed depending on the circumstances. The gospel was rather a reality that was revealed concretely in the word and suffering of the apostle, not in stupendous, abnormal demonstrations of power by a divine miracle-worker. The struggle over the apostolate which forms the unifying theme of our Second Corinthians throughout, chapters 8 and 9 not excepted (see below, pp. 108 ff.), is therefore one continuous struggle for the gospel itself. This is what makes the assurance Paul received from the Lord, "My grace is all you need; power comes to its full strength in weakness" (12:9), more than a personal consolation for the apostle. It is the saving message in a nutshell.

Galatians and Philippians

The letters to the Galatians and Philippians, like the Letter to Philemon already mentioned (see above, pp. 77 f.), probably belong to the same period, ca. 52–55, when Paul was staying at Ephesus. Once again Acts gives an entirely different picture of Paul's activity in this famous metropolis of Asia Minor, and of the highly intensive character and far-reaching effects of his work there. Despite the impressiveness of its account, Acts tells us nothing of his sufferings at Ephesus, but we need only look at the long list of tribulations in 2 Cor. 11:23–33. These belong to the same period, which was one of unremitting travels, trials, hardships, and persecutions. In this passage Paul gives a list of his "heroic deeds," which he contrasts with the braggings of his Corinthian opponents. The controversial Letter to the Galatians belongs to the same context. Like the Corinthian correspondence, this too was triggered by wandering "Christian" preachers, whose false doctrine, however, was different from that at Corinth inasmuch as it involved Judaizing observances. Contrary to the Pauline gospel, these false preachers held that to be a true Christian a Gentile must accept circumcision and thus be incorporated into the privileged Jewish people of God, and must obey the law like proselytes from paganism converted by Jewish missionaries. Appealing as they had no right to do to the original apostles in Jerusalem, these false teachers accused Paul of arbitrary behavior and of preaching a truncated version of the gospel.

Unfortunately their calumnies fell on willing ears. The newcomers seemed to be received as legitimate preachers. They were regarded as the true radicals, and Paul was the man of compromise. Faced with these charges, Paul outlines for the first time his teaching on the law and justification by faith alone. This brings Galatians rather close to Romans.

More personal and less didactic is the Letter to the Philippians. This, too, is probably a collection of several short letters written by Paul from prison to a community with which he was on exceptionally familiar terms. Frequent exchanges between the prisoner and his correspondents are presupposed throughout the "letter," thus suggesting that Paul wrote from a prison in Ephesus, which was not far from Philippi, rather than in Rome or Caesarea. Although Luke does not mention this particular imprisonment—another gap in his narrative—the Corinthian correspondence contains hints of an imprisonment at Ephesus (1 Cor. 15: 32; 2 Cor. 1:8 f.). Despite the anxious situation and the uncertain result of the court action which Paul was facing

(Phil. 1:19 ff.), he writes throughout in a cheerful mood (1:18; 2:27 f.; 3:1; 4:4, 10). At the same time he issues a stern warning against false teachers (3:2 ff.) of a Jewish gnostic character. This makes Philippians one of the most important documents on the doctrine of justification.

Romans

But Paul's most mature expression of this doctrine occurs in Romans. This lengthy and important letter occupies a special place among Paul's letters and has exercised a profound influence in church history. Unlike the other letters, it is addressed to a community Paul did not know, for the church at Rome was founded not by him but by anonymous Christians at a very early date.

The main difference between this letter and the rest lies in the almost complete lack of reference to concrete news, or to the experiences and problems of his correspondents. Instead Romans gives the impression of a clear and orderly "compendium of Christian doctrine" (Melanchthon) consisting of general and timeless truths unconnected with any specific situation.

Many of the themes in Romans are already scattered about in 1 and 2 Corinthians, Galatians, and Philippians, which were written a short time before. But in those letters the themes in question were interspersed with statements and admonitions slanted to particular events, problems, and errors in the various communities and occasioned in some instances by the arrival of false teachers who were causing disturbances and attacking the Pauline gospel. But there is nothing of this in the Letter to the Romans. What Paul does here is to think through the basic principles of his doctrine of justification. He relates these principles to one another and carries them to a logical conclusion, bringing them into focus where they had previously appeared in scattered fragments. This is why Romans is rightly regarded as the Magna Charta of the apostle's theology.

But Romans offers no complete doctrinal system. For example it never mentions the Last Supper (1 Cor. 10–11), nor is there anything to correspond with the broad discussion on the resurrection of the dead or the Parousia as in 1 Corinthians 15. But the number of specific themes it touches on is amazing. We can mention here only the most important.

There is a programmatic formulation of the gospel in the opening chapter (1:16 f.), followed by a lengthy and moving discussion of the fallen state of all mankind, Jew and pagan alike standing under the condemnation of the law (1:18–3:20; cf. Gal. 3–4; 1 Cor. 1:21). Then there is the comparison between Adam and Christ: Adam's fall was the beginning and origin of sin and death, which spread to all men, and Christ is the head of a new and redeemed humanity (Rom. 5:12 ff.; cf. 1 Cor. 15:21, 45). Paul explains how the believers are justified by the sacrificial death of Christ, and portrays Abraham as the father and prototype of a new and redeemed people of God (Rom. 3–4; cf. Gal. 3–4). He speaks of baptism and the new life (Rom. 6; cf. Gal. 3: 27 f.), of the mission of the Son of God and the assurance of those who are called to be sons of God through his Spirit (Rom. 8; cf. Gal. 4). He describes the community as the one body of Christ with many members (Rom. 12:3 ff.; cf. 1 Cor. 12). He talks about the "strong" and the "weak" in this community in order to counter the selfishness and rivalry which was marring its life (Rom. 14–15; cf. 1 Cor. 8–10).

Each of these themes was adumbrated in the earlier letters, many of them in a context of urgency while Paul was fighting for the truth of the gospel. But in Romans they are developed in a systematic way. Given the far-reaching, worldwide sweep of the apostle's thinking in this letter, it is no accident that it contains the first mention of his plans to extend his missionary work as far as Rome and Spain.

All of this is matched by the intensity which marks this writing and this writing only, where Paul reflects systematically on the situation of mankind as a whole. No other letter is so rich in its themes or so illuminating for Pauline anthropology. Man is God's creation in the midst of this world. He is a corporeal being, created with heart, spirit, conscience, and reason, and intended for communion with God. But man has misused these endowments to rebel against his Creator. He has become aggressive in his constant urge for self-assertion (sin), perhaps especially in his "religious" behavior. In everything he does man is led by the "flesh," that is to say, he acts for self-realization. Because of this he has fallen into bondage and lives under the curse of the powers of evil. He wants to live and yet he is a child of death, destined for death by his greed for life. Nowhere else in the letters, and nowhere else in ancient literature, Greek or Jewish, is there such a penetrating description of man's plight and contradiction as in Rom. 7:7–25. Nor is there any other writing which speaks so forcefully of the power of grace to set man free to live the new life of faith.

Paul even deals in Romans with the concrete questions of daily living (12–15). Here he pulls together many of the more important pronouncements he had formulated previously, ignoring the variations in language and outlook which had formerly characterized them when they were first addressed to pagan or Jewish readers.

In Romans, Galatians, and Philippians what we have is mainly the language of justification, originally coined to counteract Jewish ideas of salvation but here transposed into a different key so as to make it intelligible to Gentile Christians and help them realize that they too had a share in it. It was because of transposition that Paul could expect the Gentile Christians in Rome to accept it also.

But why does Paul write the letter at all, and to the Romans of all people? Although the document is mainly doctrinal, and hardly refers to concrete questions in the community in Rome, there is one exception, the conflict between the "strong" and the "weak" (Rom. 14–15), the treatment of which is obviously modeled after 1 Corinthians 8–10. We know there must have been an occasion for this letter as there was for all the others. This is shown by a few statements in Rom. 15:14–33, which a superficial reading could easily misconstrue as merely a piece of information, an announcement of the "travel plans" customary in letters.

For a long time Paul had been planning to embark upon a new field of labor in the west, but again and again he had been forced to postpone it. Now, after concluding his mission in the eastern half of the empire, he has to go up to Jerusalem to deliver the collection. It was, as he himself admits, a dangerous project whose outcome was highly uncertain. He expects to be persecuted by the Jews. This is understandable, for the Jews of Jerusalem, like those in the diaspora, had in the meantime come to regard Paul as a notorious enemy of the law and a blasphemer against God.

Strangely enough, however, he also feared resistance from the original community at Jerusalem. They might refuse to accept the collection, even though it had been agreed upon at the apostolic conference six or seven years previously and

Paul had not only undertaken the task with enthusiasm but also accomplished it successfully (1 Cor. 16:3 f.; 2 Cor. 8–9). This suggests that the collection was intended not merely for the relief of economic and social need. Otherwise, how could the "poor" in Jerusalem have refused it? It was actually an expression of the solidarity between Gentiles and Jews and a demonstration of the legitimacy of Paul's preaching of the gospel free from the law.

By the time Romans was written, however, this solidarity could no longer be taken for granted in the original Jerusalem community. Since the apostolic conference, James, the Lord's brother, a Jewish Christian (Gal. 2:11 ff.), had taken over the leadership. The community had grown through the accession of Jewish converts and had adopted a Jewish type of constitution. It was increasingly troubled by conflicts (Acts 12:1 ff.) with official non-Christian Judaism, and compelled as a result to demonstrate its fidelity to law and tradition. In the meantime the Gentile Christian communities had grown by leaps and bounds, with the result that the Palestinian community was no longer willing to accept Paul's Gentile Christians on equal terms, or to tolerate his mission without question. This explains why Paul had to be prepared for reluctance on the part of the church in Jerusalem. They might be unwilling to go along with his demonstration of the solidarity of Jews and Gentiles. They might refuse to accept the collection.

The information on which Luke's account is based (Acts 21:15 ff.) is enough to indicate the change in the situation and the tensions that ensued. The battle over the old question of Judaism versus Christianity and of the old versus the new understanding of salvation would have to be fought all over again. Of course, we must not accept Luke's later view of history uncritically. He is still aware of Paul's last journey to Jerusalem, and even gives the names of Paul's companions (20:4). Much of the detail about the more intimate circumstances and the places where Paul stopped en route is quite plausible. But of the collection Luke had only the vaguest notion. He was oblivious of the fact that it was the main purpose of the journey and alludes to it only once in passing (24:17). And what he does say about it is notoriously mistaken. He thinks it was a personal gift from Paul to his fellow Jews and a proof of Paul's fidelity to the law.

But if we take our clue from Paul himself in Rom. 15: 25 ff. and 2 Corinthians 8–9, we can see why Paul could not allow anyone else to deliver the collection for him (1 Cor. 16:3 f.) and thus be freed to proceed directly from Corinth to his new field of labor in the west. Paul had to be ready to defend his preaching to the Gentiles, and their freedom from the law, as he had done earlier at the conference, and to argue his case again. But this time he would have to do so under far more difficult circumstances, both external and internal.

As always, Paul's paramount concern was for the bond of unity between the already established and still growing Gentile church and the church at Jerusalem, where the Christ event, the turning point in world history, originated. The bonds which linked the church and the unbelieving Jewish people were no less important. The Jews had been chosen by an act of God's saving will. He had blessed them and made them the instrument of his promise. These bonds were a fact of both secular history and salvation history. After all, from its very beginning Israel had been called and destined for life through the grace of God alone. Since it had become hardened, the gospel must meanwhile go to the Gentiles, whose acceptance of the saving message had put Israel to shame. But this was only a detour. Paul was confident that salvation would again return to the people of Israel. This is the great theme of the remarkable section in Romans 9–11.

The Letter to the Romans is a powerful expression of the apostle's thinking as he contemplated the impending confrontation in Jerusalem, the last he would have to face. It is not hard to see why Paul was so anxious to share his thoughts with the Romans. The outcome of the negotiations in Jerusalem would be crucial for the predominantly Gentile Christian community in Rome, as well as for his own further missionary work. That is why he begs them help him with their prayers (15:30 ff.).

Paul's hopes were not fulfilled, and what he feared actually came to pass. His journey to Jerusalem led to his imprisonment and death. Acts comes to an end before the death of Paul (21–28), though it hints at it unmistakably (20:25 ff.; 21:4, 11 ff.). As things turned out, Romans was the last of Paul's letters, in fact his last will and testament.

APPENDIX: *The Deutero-Pauline Letters*

Although controverted, misinterpreted, and largely forgotten, the heritage of the apostle was preserved by his disciples and followers, though not without modifications at certain points. Proof of this is to be found in the deutero-Pauline letters, letters which circulated under his name, claimed his authority, and were eventually included in the canon as authentic Pauline material. The pseudonymity of these letters, as of other writings having the names of other apostles attached to them, must not be measured by our modern laws of authorship and copyright or our own ideas of morality. There were no such laws in antiquity, and it is particularly unfair to apply our modern criteria to these early Christian writings. For the names chosen for attachment represent not so much their individuality of personal outlook as their authority in connection with revelation, teaching, and tradition. This of course is not to deny that there are also instances of crude forgery among the writings of this type.

An early example of the attempt to bring the Pauline heritage to bear upon a false enthusiasm can be seen in the Second Letter to the Thessalonians (see above, p. 93). Two letters purporting to be written by Paul from prison, the letters to the Colossians and to the Ephesians, must also be included among the deutero-Paulines. Both contain genuine Pauline thoughts, and the letter to Colossae (Phrygia) is very close to the Letter to Philemon so far as external circumstances are concerned. The letter to Ephesus is quite different. There is nothing in it to suggest the intimate relationship between Paul and a community he had worked in for so many years. It could just as well have been addressed to any other community, which is one of the arguments against its authenticity.

The two letters are closely related in style and content. Parts of Ephesians read like a commentary on Colossians. They take up some of Paul's favorite notions, modify them in a characteristic way, and develop them in an entirely different direction, so much so that we are justified in thinking that both letters were written by pupils of Paul. Even the style is different from the genuinely Pauline letters. The sentences are inordinately lengthy. They consist of meditations constantly interrupted by a flood of parentheses, synonyms, and parallel turns of phrase. There are numerous fragments of hymns, and other liturgical snippets. The language, outlook, and theological peculiarities of both distinguish these letters from the genuine letters of Paul. Of course there are plenty of references to the great themes of his theology (justification, reconciliation, the community as the body of Christ, baptism, new life, and resurrection). But the accents are different, the emphasis shifted, and the perspectives and dimensions changed. Then there is another point, the obvious borrowings—and sometimes refutation—of images and motifs from other religions. This is explicitly the case with Colossians, which argues vehemently against gnostic "philosophy" (2:8 ff., 16 ff., 20 ff.), and implicitly the case in Ephesians, which however is devoid of polemics.

The thought of both letters moves in ever widening circles, embracing the whole cosmos with all its spheres and powers. It speaks about the mystery of Christ that has been revealed (Col. 1:26 f.; 2:2; 4:3; Eph. 1:9; 3:3 f., 9 ff.): the reconciliation of the universe through the death of Christ on the cross (Col. 1:20; Eph. 1:7, 10), his triumph over all powers opposed to God (Col. 2:15; Eph. 1:21 f.), Christ as the "peace" between God and mankind whereby God has broken down the wall of partition, abolishing the differences between the people of the promise (Jews) and the aliens (Gentiles) so that all have received equal rights of citizenship. This central Pauline understanding is the principal theme of Ephesians (2:15 ff.). The faithful are translated into this perfect state of salvation through baptism.

All these thoughts are proclaimed and unfolded in spatial categories rather than, as with Paul, in temporal and eschatological imagery. Thus the Pauline motif of the church as the body of Christ is enlarged into the image of Christ as "the head of the body," the church whose members grow in grace toward him who is now exalted in heaven (Col. 1:18; 2:10; Eph. 1:22; 4:15). This must find visible expression in the behavior of the faithful "in the Lord," as the ethical exhortations in both letters put it.

The Pastoral Letters, ostensibly addressed to Paul's fellow laborers Timothy and Titus, come from a later phase in the struggle against heresy. Unlike Ephesians and Colossians, which show originality in the cosmic dimensions of their thought, these documents are of a completely different type. Their vision is restricted to the "intermediate sphere of the Church," as Ulrich Wilckens puts it. They are also clearly distinguishable in both language and character from the genuinely Pauline letters. The letters to Timothy and Titus too purport to be writings of the apostle. They contain echoes of Pauline formulas and phraseology, and they reproduce Pauline utterances in the form of propositional statements. There are also plenty of biographical details and references to particular situations, drawn from various traditions which can no longer be identified. Presumably these details are intended to create a stronger impression of authenticity. They have little connection with what the writings actually intend to say, except in the case of Second Timothy, which purports to be the last will and testament of the apostle, written as he lay in chains waiting for death.

Above all, the Pastorals provide a picture of the important process by which the apostle's teaching was transmitted to his successors. This in itself is enough to show that all three of them are official letters rather than private communications. They are nominally addressed to Timothy and Titus, persons who, having been authorized and installed in office by the laying on of hands, really stand for the church as a whole. It is their task in turn to ordain in their appointed spheres of labor other worthy men to serve as bishops and deacons of the community.

As regards the form of these letters, the most important portions should be classed as church orders, written in the postapostolic age. For example, in 1 Tim. 3:1 ff. we have a "mirror" for bishops and deacons. Other parts consist of fixed doctrinal formulas to be passed on to others (1 Tim. 3:16; 2 Tim. 2:8). Then there are general directives reflecting a bourgeois ideal of Christian morality.

The Pastorals are devoid of philosophical reflection. Their sole aim is to preserve wholesome and pure doctrine, practical Christian behavior in everyday life, and good housekeeping, so to speak. It is not by accident that rules for conduct are interspersed with passages about worship and ministry. The latter consist entirely of general "household codes."

The purpose of these letters is to place the church upon a firm foundation in order to protect it from the heresy of gnosis. There are numerous denunciations of this heresy, and the true office-bearer and Christian is forbidden to get involved in any discussion of its weird and speculative mythology.

All this is enough to show that Paul could not possibly have been the author of these "letters," either directly or indirectly. He could not have dictated them, nor could he have communicated what he wanted to say to a "secretary" by word of mouth, leaving the secretary free to write it up later and give it its final form. The difference in outlook and theology is too obvious and the condition of the church, its constitution and its tendencies, all point to a later date.

Nevertheless the value of the Pastorals lies not so much in their general outlook as in the tradition they have collected and preserved. Theirs was an age of confusion, and the temptation to error was strong. But these letters are straight-forward, clear, and definite. In the helpful guidelines they provided for the community and for the individual they have preserved a good deal of the Pauline heritage.

4. The Later Writings of the New Testament

UNDERSTANDING THE LATER WRITINGS

Christianity in the late first century tends to be overshadowed by the glorious era of its earliest days—the age of Jesus and the first preaching of the gospel. It is summarily dismissed as the age of the epigones. The same thing is true of the writings of that period. Unfortunately this assessment does less than justice to this "third" generation of Christianity. The very name "subapostolic," though not exactly wrong, has a somewhat pejorative connotation. Quite unintentionally, we associate it with Luke's idealized picture of the first epoch of the church, which is quite inaccurate. The characterization of the later New Testament writings as the products of "early catholicism" is equally open to objection. It is only too easy to fall into the trap of projecting back into the New Testament the idea of the church, with its doctrine and tradition, ministerial office and succession, as an institution purveying salvation. The fact is that the institutionalization of the church came later. There was never any such uniform development during the first century.

We would therefore do well not to censure the later writings in the New Testament canon by the theological standards of the previous age, or even of a later one. The historical significance of the late first century deserves to be investigated for its own sake. The decades we have in mind saw the development of a kind of specifically Christian literature, including writings of many different types and varying worth, none of them claiming canonical status. It is worth noting that none is a missionary writing; they all assume that those who will receive them are Christians.

As we have seen, this is the period in which the Gospels and the deutero-Pauline writings were written. This is also very probably the period in which the authentic Pauline epistles began to be collected and circulated beyond the communities to which they were originally addressed. Significantly, writings were composed at this time which were no longer addressed to particular communities but to a wider public, which is why the ancient church spoke of them as "catholic" epistles. Seven documents fall into this category: James, First and Second Peter, Jude, and the three Johannine letters. The last three of course were added to this group by mistake, for First John is not a letter at all and Second and Third John are not addressed to the general public. It would be easier to call Ephesians, which is ascribed to Paul, a "catholic" letter. The same is true of Hebrews—also regarded as Pauline by the ancient church—even though, except for its conclusion (13:18 ff.), it has none of the characteristics of a letter. Too, the Revelation of John begins and ends like a letter and claims in fact to be a "letter from heaven." And although the letters to the seven churches are separately addressed (2–3), the sacred number seven suggests that these churches represent a higher, ideal unity.

For all their differences, certain common experiences and tendencies have left their traces in these later New Testament writings. First and foremost, we note the distance between the time in which they were written and the period of Christian beginnings. The authors try to compensate for this by the device of pseudonymity. Two of the letters purport to be by James and Jude, the brothers of the Lord. Similarly, the two letters of Peter claim the authority of the first of the apostles. We have already seen the same thing happening in the case of the deutero-Pauline writings (see above, pp. 111 ff.). The consolidation of doctrine and faith in tradition is a remarkable feature of these writings while the apostolic legitimation of ecclesiastical office also acquires importance (Pastorals; Acts 20:18 ff.).

An obvious characteristic of these late first century writings is the way they seek to anchor the church's doctrine and faith in tradition. It becomes important to secure apostolic sanction for the church's ministry (the Pastoral Letters; Acts 20:18 ff.). Another factor closely connected with this is the constant threat of false teachers. There are repeated warnings against false prophets, often singled out as a sign of eschatological tribulation (Jude 17 ff.; 2 Pet. 2:10 ff.; 3:2 ff.; 1 John 2:18 ff.; 4:1 ff.; 5:1, 5 ff.; Heb. 13:9 ff.; cf. also Mark 13:22; Matt. 7:15 ff.; Acts 20:29 ff.; 1 Tim. 1:4; 4:3; 6:20; 2 Tim. 2:18; Titus 3:9 f.). Unlike the authentic Paul, these authors make no attempt to refute heretical doctrines by argument but denounce them summarily as corrupt and dangerous, piling up opprobrious epithets of every kind.

Furthermore, many passages speak of dire external persecution and of similar sufferings to be expected in the future (2 Tim. 2:8; Heb. 10:32 ff.; 12:7 f.; 1 Pet. 4:1 ff., 12 ff.; 5:8 f.; Rev. 2–3; 13:7 ff.).

THE CHURCH LETTERS

James

In the various Christian writings of the late first century the development and theological assimilation of Christian faith is as different as it can be. In the Letter of James faith is relegated so far into the background that we are tempted to ask if this letter was originally a Christian writing at all. Only twice in the entire writing—which is a letter in form only, being addressed "to the twelve tribes in the diaspora" —does the name of Jesus Christ appear (1:1; 2:1). In other ways, too, James is quite uninterested in reflecting theologically upon the event of salvation. Only at 5:7 ff. is there a reference to the imminent return of the Lord, but in terms no different from those in which any Jew would speak of the Day of Judgment.

Instead, interest focuses upon the practice of godly living. This is the subject of a loosely knit series of injunctions and warnings, often linked by a catchword, which deal with such things as resistance to temptation (1:2 ff.); hearing the word of God and doing it (1:19 ff.); snobbery and charitableness, especially of the rich toward the poor (2:1 ff.); and thoughtless gossip and deceptive self-assurance (3:1 ff.; 4:13 ff.). The very frequency of the imperatives—there are no less than fifty-four in 108 verses—shows that this letter is an ethical exhortation. It borrows ideas from Hellenistic-Jewish wisdom literature, without any interest whatever in the particularities of salvation history. It combines Christian sayings with Hellenistic-Gentile morality. The only theological passage is the polemic about faith and works (2:14–26). There can be no question that this discussion presupposes the Pauline teaching on justification by faith alone, albeit in a bowdlerized version. Nowhere did the apostle himself advocate a "dead" faith like that which James is combating. But this does not alter the fact that when he gets to the subject of justification, James adopts a true Jewish point of view with his emphasis on faith *and* works.

First Peter

First Peter is far more loyal to the Christian message of salvation. Like James it contains a great number of ethical injunctions. But they are embedded and anchored in the promise of the grace of God which the faithful have already received and which awaits them in the hereafter. Thus, as in the ethical parts of the Pauline letters, the indicative comes before the imperative, and the new being of Christians is the basis of all the admonitions about brotherly love within the community and toward the outside world. Redeemed by the sacrificial death of Christ (1:18 ff.) and born again through his resurrection to a living hope (1:3 ff.), Christians live under the protection of "faith" (1:5). True, here on earth they do not yet walk by sight (1:8); they are tested by suffering (1:6 f.) like aliens in a foreign land (2:11). Yet they are God's chosen race, his people, claimed by him for his own possession (2:9), and the spiritual temple of Christ (2:5). On these grounds, the "letter" admonishes its readers to show sincere affection toward their fellow Christians (1:22 ff.; 3:8; 4:8). They must be self-controlled (2:11) and humble-minded (3:8; 5:5 f.), and behave irreproachably in the midst of the pagan world around them (2:12). They must submit to rulers, who are ordained by God (2:13 ff.). They must patiently suffer injustice after the example of Christ (2:18 ff.) and be prepared for martyrdom in time of persecution (4:12 ff.). There is nothing remarkable about such experiences—they are part and parcel of the life of discipleship. This is what is meant by follow-

ing in the steps of the Lord (2:21). It is a ground for re-
joicing as the believer advances toward the inheritance that
will soon be his in heaven (1:4 ff.). The expectation that
the world will soon come to an end and the day of salvation
dawn is still as strong as ever (4:7). It is a sure goal, just
as important for the true understanding of the Christian life
as the fact that salvation is already present in Christ (1:6–
12).

In language and outlook the First Letter of Peter contains
a good deal of material which was formulated earlier. In the
opening chapters especially there are a surprising number of
allusions to baptism. Since Christ has risen from the dead
the readers are addressed as men and women who have been
born anew through the eternal, life-giving word of God
(1:3, 22 ff.; 2:2). Before this they wandered like lost sheep,
but now they have returned to the "Shepherd and Guardian"
of their souls (2:25). There is a direct reference to baptism
in 3:20 ff., where we are told that baptism has its Old
Testament counterpart in the deliverance of Noah from the
flood.

Some scholars have gone so far as to suppose that First
Peter is based on a baptismal homily. This, however, is unlikely, though as we have seen, the baptismal allusions are
unmistakable.

Other fragments of earlier tradition can also be distinguished in the "letter." There are creedlike statements and
hymns (2:21 ff.; 3:18 ff.), liturgical formulas, "household
codes" embedded in ethical exhortations (2:18 ff.; 3:1 ff.;
5:1 ff.), and Old Testament quotations scattered all over the
letter.

Anyone looking for original ideas in this writing will fail
to do it justice. All the more evident is the treasure of ex-

periences and insights of faith which it has collected and enshrined. In its many simple affirmations the letter has faithfully preserved the tradition.

This document, written for the comfort and admonition of the faithful, can hardly have been written by Peter. This is clear from the fact that the author never speaks of his connection with the earthly Jesus. Moreover, he writes in cultured Greek and is addressing Gentile Christians in Asia Minor (1:14, 18; 2:9 f.; 4:3 f.), including those living in areas which had been evangelized by Paul. Indeed, there are echoes of Pauline theology in First Peter.

Also suggestive of a later date is the picture given of governmental persecution. It is no longer local in character but originates from Rome, referred to by the code name of "Babylon" (5:13; cf. Rev. 14:8; 16:19; 17:5; 18:2 ff.). First Peter is pseudonymous, and was probably written during the reign of Domitian (A.D. 81–96).

Hebrews

The so-called Letter to the Hebrews belongs to the same period. Of all the New Testament writings, including the Revelation of John, this perhaps is the one which the modern reader finds the strangest and most difficult to understand. Yet it is worth rediscovering, a task not made easy by the fact that it defies classification. The early church tried to modify its unusual character somewhat by classifying it with the letters, on the ground of its ending (13:18–25). Because of its extensive use of the Old Testament the early church also concluded that it must have been written to a group of Jewish Christians (Hebrews). This suggestion, however, is untenable, since it is not really a letter at all. It has no preliminaries, and there are no circumstantial allusions to any particular community. It looks much more like a doctrinal treatise in the form of a sermon.

Nor is it written specifically for Jewish Christians. Some passages seem to suggest that the author was thinking of converts from paganism. The primer of Christian teaching, speaking as it does of conversion to the one true God (6:1 f.; cf. also 11:6), and the warning against apostasy (3:12) would be more suitable for former pagans. Christians everywhere accepted the Old Testament as Holy Scripture, so the author could look for Gentiles to understand him quite as much as Jews. Nor is it probable that this "letter" was written by Paul as was once widely supposed. It is quite independent in both language and outlook.

The picture of the community to which Hebrews is addressed is clear and definite, though typical of a later generation. People are instructed in the faith and baptized. They are in possession of the Bible (the Old Testament) and a creed, and they hold services of worship. But the preaching of the word has lost its excitement and they have become dull of hearing (5:11). They are threatened with hardness of heart (3–4), carelessness (12:12 ff.), boredom (10:25), even with apostasy (3:12; 4:1), and are in danger of drifting like a boat which has lost its rudder (2:1).

Faced with this situation, the preacher recalls the members of the community to their confession. But he does not content himself with appeals and exhortations or merely go on repeating what they already know. Instead, he seeks to broaden and deepen their understanding of the faith they have already held for a long time.

Hebrews develops its argument with constant reference to the Old Testament. This argument has two aspects, one christological, the other ecclesiological. Christ is the eternal high priest, and the community is the wandering people of God. The two themes are closely interwoven, indeed they are basically the same theme under two different aspects, unfolded alternately in doctrinal exposition and moral exhortation. The total saving event is summarized by the christological title of high priest, which is taken from Psalm 110. The Son of God descended to the lowest depths for man's salvation. He became one of us and was exposed as we are to temptation and sin, fear and death (2:6–18; 5:7 ff.). But God raised him to be the author of salvation. By this paradoxical path of obedience Christ ended the curse of human bondage and opened up the road to heaven (7:27; 9:12; 10:10), giving us access to God (4:14 ff.; 8:1 ff.; 10:19 ff.). Now he rules over us forever as the great high priest.

This provides the members of the community with a goal to hope for. At the same time it brings home to them a dread of apostasy like that to which Israel succumbed of old (3–4). This explains the crucial importance Hebrews attaches to faith. Faith means obedience to the word and call of God, unfaltering hope and endurance year in, year out (11). Faith is not merely the appropriate attitude of man to God. It has an objective sense. Faith demonstrates the certainty of salvation hoped for and the reality of things unseen, compared with which all things visible are unreal and transitory. This is the meaning of the preacher's "definition" of faith (11:1), the first and only time the New Testament offers such a definition.

Faith thus understood is illustrated in the great chapter that follows by means of reference to the cloud of witnesses who preceded the Christian community in the course of salvation history. But it is ultimately grounded in Jesus "on whom faith depends from start to finish" (12:2).

With its strange and tortuous arguments, Hebrews makes considerable use of the exegetical methods of Hellenistic Judaism as they are known to us from Philo of Alexandria. The influence of gnosis and its dualism is equally obvious. Bound however by Old Testament–Jewish and Christian tradition, Hebrews refuses to abandon its belief that the world is God's creation. It also interprets salvation and redemption as a release from sin—unlike gnosis, which has a lot to say about predestination and fate but nothing about sin and repentance. Hebrews also combines two quite different modes of thought, one which is timeless and the other which is temporal and eschatological. Fundamental to the theology of Hebrews is the revelation of God in the Old Testament, which points forward to the future and is full of promise but which at the same time represents a cultic order of constantly repeated observances that will be done away with— as an example of the vain observances found in all human religion. The Old Testament is transcended and abolished by the new covenant of God, by the heavenly sanctuary and the all-sufficient sacrifice of Jesus the great high priest (7–10; 12).

In many ways Hebrews comes close to Paul, for instance in the way it interprets the Christ event and in what it says of faith. Both authors reject the Jewish understanding of salvation. Both speak of the old and new covenants. Both insist that the old law has been superseded as the way to salvation (Heb. 8:13). Hebrews, however, is interested only in the cultic law of the Old Testament, which Paul almost entirely ignores; it never thinks in terms of justification like the apostle. Thus, despite all its strangeness, Hebrews represents an independent and far-reaching theological achievement expressed in language of amazing power.

Jude and Second Peter

Jude and Second Peter are hardly to be mentioned in the same breath as Hebrews. They are both spirited defenses of traditional faith, threatening the errors of heresy with well-deserved judgment. Jude claims to be a letter written by the brother of the Lord. It makes its point with a long list of God's punishments on evildoers in the Old Testament. Second Peter is an expansion of Jude (2), but directed against the denial of the Parousia. It is no more than a rearguard action based on an appeal to the pure doctrine of the apostles, especially that of Peter, with traditional apologetic arguments loosely strung together. It is no accident that the letter makes so much of its fictitious claim to Petrine authorship. Its portrayal of the heretics follows the usual pattern of denunciation.

Its eschatology has an air of orthodox teaching but is inadequately developed in theological terms. It is distinctly inferior to Paul's eschatology, and even to that of First Peter and Hebrews. It is no longer the expression of a living faith. Not even the few impressive phrases it contains are enough to deceive the reader. As we take a closer look at its appeal to the apostles and its memories of their past glories, we get the impression of a venerable company of orthodox veterans being thrown into the firing line.

The date of Second Peter is quite late, somewhere in the middle of the second century, which makes it the latest document in the New Testament.

THE REVELATION OF JOHN

The book of Revelation is an entirely different matter. It is the last outburst of eschatological excitement in early Christianity, not another stubborn defense of traditional doctrine. It has long been, to use its own words though not in the sense in which they were originally intended, "a book sealed with seven seals," and as such has generally been left to the sects. But the author meant the words to be taken in exactly the opposite way: his is a book with *open* seals, *unveiling* the secrets of the end which the seer wrote down at the behest and dictation of the risen Christ. The communities of Asia Minor addressed in the seven letters of chapters 2–3 stand for the whole Christian church (2:7, 11, 17).

We shall miss its meaning if we think that the book fell down from heaven as a direct message for our own day— which is how sects such as Jehovah's Witnesses understand it. If we are to make sense of Revelation at all we must let it remain in its own time, with its own religious and historical background, strange though it is to us. Its very first word, "revelation" (apocalypse), places it explicitly in the tradition, outlook, and literary genre of contemporary Jewish apocalyptic. Apocalyptic is a later form of Old Testament prophecy which still bears the marks of its origin, with its extensive quotations, images, and phrases from the Old Testament prophets. But apocalyptic differs from prophecy by virtue of the cosmic dualism in which its expectation of the end is couched. Its great themes, portrayed in an endless succession of scenes, images, and speculations, are the end of the world, the Last Judgment, and the inauguration of the new heaven and the new earth. The importance of apocalyptic for the whole of early Christianity can hardly be overestimated, even though it was modified when taken over, sometimes in a positive way, sometimes critically. Jewish apocalyptic provides us with the clue to understanding the fantastic thoughts and archaic language of the Revelation of John.

Yet there is more in this book than a heritage of religion and theology revived from oblivion by an odd character with a taste for eschatological speculation. John writes in the midst of an acute historical crisis, probably during the reign of Domitian, in the mid-nineties, when the conflict between the church and the pagan state flared up and unleashed terrible persecution upon the Christians. The seer himself was a victim of persecution, apparently in exile on the island of Patmos (1:9). He wrote to encourage his brethren in the faith and to urge them to continued loyal witness. He was caught up in a trance and inspired to discern the counsels of God. So he tries to make sense of the community's suffering and to explain what is happening in the history of their times. He assures them that Christ will soon return.

We can see both the close affinities between the book of Revelation and the Jewish and early Christian apocalyptic, and the differences between them. In the use of apocalyptic patterns, in the way he introduces himself, in the imagery and symbolism he employs, and in his arrangement of the visions, creating the impression of a continuous succession of events, the seer is a creature of his age. This is true even though he tells us his own name and refuses to hide behind the name of some famous man of God in ancient times. Like other apocalyptists, he makes use of sources and earlier traditions. He often employs the device of sacred numbers. There are seven letters to the churches (2–3), and the visions occur in a series of seven: seven seals, seven trumpets, and seven bowls (6–7; 8–11; 15–16). The Revelation of John was not written in an ecstatic trance any more than other contemporary apocalypses.

What distinguishes this work from other Jewish and Christian documents of the same genre is its interpretation of history. It is impossible to press the sequence of events into an ordered pattern or to treat this work like a railroad schedule listing the stations and predicting the course of future events until the end of the world. Rather, there are three successive accounts of the same history. First, the vision of the seals gives a summary sketch (the scroll written on both sides which the exalted Christ holds in his hands); it can be read in its entirety only when the last seal has been broken (5:1; 8:1). Then come the trumpet visions; here the picture is a little clearer but still fragmentary and allusive. Only in the bowl visions and their sequel (15:1–22:5) does the whole scheme become clear and comprehensible.

At first sight, this scheme looks like nothing more than a refined technique of composition. In fact, however, it is the very heart of the author's message. The world is in rebellion against God. This rebellion manifests itself in the hardness of men's hearts and their arrogance under the blows of God's judgment. The whole process gets worse and worse, until it culminates in the worship of the Roman emperor and the power of the state. There is universal chaos, and soon a terrible war is launched against the "holy ones" who, armed only with steadfastness and loyalty to their faith, refuse to submit. Then Rome is unmasked as Babylon, the great whore, whose bestial rage on earth is only the final fling of Satan after he has been thrown down from heaven and put to silence before God (12–13). God had already decided what to do with the world when he sent Christ to bring salvation and peace. That is why the great vision of the enthronement of the lamb that was slain comes at the beginning, not at the end, as in other apocalyptic texts of the New Testament (Mark 13:26 ff.; 2 Thess. 2:8 ff.). It is Christ who decides the world's destiny; he alone is worthy to take the book of life from the hand of God and open its seal, thus bringing the world's history to its climax. Amid all the terrors of the end there is one question that keeps resounding: Who will be able to stand (6:17)? But the faithful have the promise already here and now. They are the true people of God whom he has redeemed (7:9 ff.; 14:1 ff.; 19:1 ff.). They have on their foreheads the seal of God, the sign of his ownership and protection. They are on the way to a new heaven and a new earth (21–22).

Thus the Revelation of John is a potent expression of the Christian message, though its doctrine of the church is admittedly a narrow one. Ecclesiology has almost become a theology of history, overgrown with fantastic speculations.

THE FOURTH GOSPEL
AND THE JOHANNINE LETTERS

The Fourth Gospel is so unique that it almost defies classification among the other New Testament writings. If we give it a late date this is not due to embarrassment, as if we did not know quite what to do with it. A number of preliminary questions concerning the circumstances of its origin can in fact be answered.

Something can be said, for example, about the author of the Gospel, at least negatively: we can say who he was not. Even in the early church the question of its authorship was a subject of lively debate. Biblical critics used to call it *the* Johannine question. Today that question has lost its importance. The attribution of authorship to John bar Zebedee, for reasons that are obvious enough, goes back to the late second century. There is nothing in the Gospel itself, however, to support the view; it has in fact proven wrong for several reasons. External evidence gives us little help. All in all, it is best to let the document remain anonymous.

The Fourth Gospel can be dated with a fair degree of accuracy. In 1935 a tiny papyrus fragment from the first third of the second century was discovered in Upper Egypt. It contains a few verses from John 18, which proves that the Fourth Gospel was known in that region already at that time. On the other hand the Jesus tradition it contains is in an advanced stage of development. The same is true of its language, theology, and world of thought. All this makes it certain that the Fourth Gospel is later than the synoptics. We would therefore date it somewhere around A.D. 100. It was probably written in Syria or Asia Minor, in roughly the same area as the other New Testament writings, the synoptic Gospels included.

According to the tradition of the ancient church, the Fourth Gospel is the work of the same John who wrote the Apocalypse. But this opinion, which even today has its advocates, is untenable. The Gospel of John and the Revelation of John are poles apart in language and theology. Yet for all their differences there are certain affinities between them. They evidently emanated from communities that were similar in structure, communities which in sociological terms we might call conventicles.

The communities which figure in the book of Revelation are under the guidance of prophets inspired by the Spirit. They are not organized on hierarchical lines. This is not at all typical of the late first or early second century communities, especially in Asia Minor. Luke, the Pastorals, First Peter, Ignatius, and Polycarp all presuppose the institution of elders, bishops, and deacons in the communities. There is not a trace of any of these offices in the Gospel of John, where the Spirit is given to the whole community (20:19 ff.). Instead, we must picture the author of the Gospel as a wandering charismatic teacher, not officially attached to any local community. He is like the "elder" of the Third Letter of John (though not identical with him), who was also faced with an arrogant representative of the official ministry of the church, and had to defend himself and his colleagues with vigor.

Perhaps this is the place to mention the fact that because of its extremely individualistic outlook the Gospel of John had a hard time getting accepted into the canon. It made the grade only after revision by an early redactor.

There are other affinities between the Fourth Gospel and the book of Revelation. Both contain similiar theological motifs, even the same terms, though they understand them in a different sense and use them in a quite different way. Both speak of Christ as the Word (Logos) of God. He is the sacrificial Lamb, humiliated and exalted. Both use such terms as life and death, testimony and witness. Both attach considerable importance to eschatological and apocalyptic themes, such as the judgment of the world, the fall of Satan, and the resurrection of the dead. In both writings earthly history is interpreted in terms of realized eschatology. Common to both is their radical distinction between the Christian community and Judaism.

But in spite of their affinities, there is a great gulf between Revelation and John in language and thought. This would suggest that the apocalyptist and the evangelist were the heirs of a similar apocalyptic tradition. One accepted the tradition and passed it on intact, while the other transformed it into a thoroughgoing realized eschatology (see below, pp. 139 ff.).

The apocalyptist concentrates on the future and the present, with hardly a single reference to the earthly Jesus. The evangelist, on the other hand, focuses his attention on the earthly history of Jesus. This raises the question of his relation to the synoptists. Was John familiar with them at all? Certain common traditions, especially in the passion narrative and its associated complex, in several miracle stories (4:46 ff.; 6:1 ff., 16 ff.), and in a few scattered dominical sayings tend to suggest that he was. Yet we are still left with no more than a nucleus of common traditions about the earthly ministry and fate of Jesus, and even these vary considerably in detail. Hence it is much more likely that the fourth evangelist knew nothing of the synoptic Gospels.

If this supposition is correct, the Fourth Gospel should not be interpreted in terms of the Lucan prologue (Luke 1:1–4; see above, pp. 62 ff.), despite the natural temptation to do so. The fourth evangelist did not make a random selection from the earlier Gospels and their sources in order to produce—on a different theological basis—a revised version of the gospel history, revised especially in its treatment of the person and message of Jesus. The Johannine Gospel is not the literary successor of Mark. It is rather a complementary work, in some respects theologically related but the product of a different milieu.

Like Mark, John has incorporated earlier traditions, including certain collections already in existence. This is certainly true of the passion narrative and most likely true of the complex of seven miracle stories: the wedding at Cana

(2:1 ff.); the healing of the royal official's son (4:46 ff.); the lame man at Bethesda (5:1 ff.); the feeding of the five thousand (6:1 ff.); the walking on the water (6:16 ff.); the man born blind (9); and the raising of Lazarus (11). Compared with the synoptic miracles, the miraculous element is greatly enhanced in John. The Johannine "signs source" recalls the Hellenistic stories about divine wonder-workers. This does not apply, though, to the evangelist's portrait of Christ, however considerable the space it allots to the miraculous. Indeed, John has no hesitation in calling his Gospel a book of signs, a title which he gives right at the end of the Gospel (chapter 21 is a postscript by a later hand). These "signs" Jesus did to show that he was the Messiah and Son of God (20:30 f.).

The crucial question, however, is what John meant by signs and how he treated them. They are not stupendous deeds in the popular sense, intended to demonstrate the divine power of Jesus to nonbelievers. Their real meaning is perceptible only to faith. Their purpose is not so much to point to the miracle-worker; it is really the other way round —the signs receive their meaning from him. Unbelief constantly misunderstands them and treats them as tangible demonstrations of an earthly, transitory kind raised to a higher power. The Johannine miracle stories, like Jesus' discourses, are constantly exposed to this misunderstanding.

The true meaning of Jesus' deeds is brought out only in the revelation discourses, above all in the "I am" sayings. These sayings, the most characteristic feature of the Fourth Gospel, occur in various forms: "I am the bread of life" (6:35), says the Johannine Christ, "the light of the world" (8:12; 9:5), "the good shepherd" (10:11), "the resurrection and the life" (11:25), "the way, the truth and the life" (14:6), "the true vine" (15:1). Each of these sayings contains both a promise and an offer: what you seek, what men long for in their hunger for true love, that I am. At the same time, however, they utter a decisive no to the many substitutes for life and salvation which satisfy the world. Several of the miracles have an explicit "I am" saying attached to them (6, 9, 11). In other cases such a saying is implied though not articulated. Jesus' miracles are always transparent illustrations. They have a symbolic meaning, pointing to the works of God which Jesus performs in his capacity as the Son (5:19 ff.).

This brings us to the real theme of the Gospel, which is the divine event of revelation accomplished through the medium of the history of the earthly Jesus. The whole of John's theology, expressed in a variety of ways, revolves around Jesus as the revealer of God.

The evangelist begins not with the baptism of Jesus by John (as in Mark) or with Jesus' birth (as in Matthew and Luke), but in eternity, before all time. The prologue at the beginning of the Gospel sets out the evangelist's program. It is a hymn to the divine Logos or Word, which became flesh in Jesus. Those who believed in him saw his glory and praised him in the Logos hymn which the evangelist took over from the community's tradition, adding to it explanations of his own (1:1–18).

The prologue sheds a transcendent light on all the ensuing narratives about Jesus' earthly work, his words, and his fate. In eternal unity with the Father Jesus performs his deeds, delivers his proclamation, suffers, bears witness, and wins the victory. Sent, accredited, and attested by the Father, he is not merely a mystic who traffics in heavenly secrets. He is the Revealer, and as such the sole theme of the Gospel from start to finish.

As such, he is a stranger in the world. Although the world is God's creation and owes its life and light to him, it has always closed its eyes to the truth and opted for deceit and falsehood. Now it demonstrates its rebellion against God in its constantly renewed attacks against Jesus. The only God and Savior the world is willing to recognize is one who is prepared to accord it accreditation and to accept it on its own terms. The world's determination to assert itself is seen in its constant appeal to its hallowed religious traditions (Abraham, Moses, the Temple, Scripture). That is why the Jews always figure in the Fourth Gospel as the enemies of God par excellence, the very offspring of the devil himself (8:44). They are blind to the truth, to the reality of God as it is encountered in Jesus (9:39 ff.). They regard Jesus as a demon-possessed heretic (7:20; 8:48, 52; 10:25) whom they must get rid of lest the whole people perish (11:49; 18:14).

Hence the dualism that pervades the Gospel: truth and falsehood, life and death, light and darkness, freedom and slavery to sin. This is not the dualism of metaphysical speculation, but a dramatic conflict played out in the history of Jesus.

But is that still a real history? Certainly not, if by history we mean a series of events occurring in time. Nor is it history as presented in the earlier synoptic Gospels, which still contain a good deal of authentic Jesus tradition. There is surprisingly little factual material in John's Gospel, although it sometimes preserves reliable memories. It will not do to harmonize the synoptic and Johannine portraits of the history and figure of Jesus. There are simply too many gaps in the Fourth Gospel for that. John has nothing about the kingdom of God as Jesus proclaimed it in his parables, nothing about Jesus' interpretation of Scripture in the conflict stories, his consorting with the outcast and unclean, and the like. The dramatis personae in John are shadowy figures—more shadowy than in the synoptics—who in one way or another serve only to bear witness to Jesus. Even John the Baptist is no longer a preacher of repentance and the forerunner, but simply a witness (1:6 ff., 15, 19 ff., 29 ff., 35 ff.; 3:36 ff.). The narratives in the Fourth Gospel generally start with a scenic introduction, but then they get lost in the timeless truths of the discourses (cf. chapters 3, 5, 6). This creates the impression that the history of the earthly Jesus has been absorbed by a peculiar kind of theology.

Such an impression, however, is only partially true. There can be no question but what the Gospel of John is very different from the Jesus tradition in the synoptics. Its portrait of Christ is deeply impregnated with gnostic concepts and myths. However, it is also quite different from gnosis. It refuses to surrender its understanding of the world as God's creation. It does not treat the world as a place of chaos, in a state of rebellion against God, a chaos into which the souls of men have tragically fallen from their divine origin. John equates the world with darkness and evil because and insofar as men have deliberately cut themselves adrift from God. Salvation is not brought about by a heavenly figure of light retrieving kindred souls from an alien sphere and bringing them back into the world beyond. True, there are a few echoes of such gnostic themes. But the dominant attitude toward perdition and salvation in John's Gospel is quite different.

Above all, the redeemer is still an earthly and historical person, God's "word become flesh" in Jesus. Redemption is effected in the earthly history of Jesus, which ended in his death. But was that death the end? No, it was also a new beginning. For only with his departure from the world and his going to the Father is the redemptive work of the earthly Jesus completed (19:30) and made effective. Only then has his history really begun. Only then is it no longer a history confined to the world of time, but a divine event occurring in the present encounter of faith with Jesus and his word. In this sense the fourth evangelist has radically transposed the traditional apocalyptic eschatology of early Christianity and made it relevant to the present. He who hears Jesus' word and believes has passed from death to life; he no longer has to face judgment (5:24 f.). For Jesus himself is the "crisis" of the world. In him the sentence of life and death has been finally pronounced. Because he is the savior he is also the judge (3:16 ff.). That is why in John's Gospel the saving events which Christian doctrine otherwise distinguishes coincide (the resurrection and ascension of Jesus, the outpouring of the Spirit, and the Parousia). What takes place in all of these events is Jesus' coming for salvation and judgment.

It is evident that in this respect the timeless thinking of gnosis has influenced the Fourth Gospel. John almost seems to have abandoned Paul's passionate insistence on the "not-yet," which Paul had worked out in response to the gnostic intoxication with perfectionism (1 Cor. 15; cf. 2 Tim. 2:18). But to assume that this is actually the case would be unfair. For when John speaks of faith he does not mean the fanatical self-consciousness of the enthusiasts, who believed they had already been transported into another aeon. On the contrary, John's Gospel fully recognizes the earthly, temporal circumstances of the faithful living on in the world after Jesus' death. He pulls no punches about the situation of the believers. To human eyes time has passed Jesus by and the world still goes on. The world triumphs while the disciples have sorrow (16:20 ff.). Believers will be cast out in God's name. They will be scattered and even put to death (16:2, 32 f.). To all appearances their Lord has deserted them. They will never again see him in earthly form, any more than the world will (13:33; 16:16). But appearances deceive. For just when they seem to be deserted, Jesus gives his friends who remain on earth the promise of the Spirit, a promise which could not be fulfilled while he was still with them on earth (7:39; 16:5 ff.).

This promise is given to the disciples in the farewell discourses (13:31–17:26), which have no counterpart in the synoptic Gospels and are of unique importance for the understanding of Christ and history in the Gospel of John. The disciples are gathered for the last time around their Master on the night before his arrest. Here we have a picture of the community on earth. The community has a history of its own, but a history that is permeated by the history of Jesus now completed. The discourses are totally devoid of even the faintest trace of sadness; they are filled with the peace which passes all understanding. It makes no difference that Jesus is about to die. The discourses foretell the coming of "another Advocate," the Spirit of truth. This Spirit will reveal far more than Jesus was able to impart to his disciples before his death; the Spirit will reveal the truth in its entirety (14:16, 26; 15:26; 16:5–15). Does this mean that the Spirit will surpass Jesus and put his revelation into the shade? Strange to say, the answer is yes. For the fact is, the faithful will never see the earthly One again. Yet this other Advocate is Jesus himself in a new form. His mission completed, Jesus entered the word of proclamation, therein to return again and again to his disciples. He leaves them only to return. He does not leave them as orphans (14:18). No, his departure enables his disciples to enter into a lasting communion far richer than that which they had with him while he was still on earth. So the moment when the earthly One vanishes from their sight becomes the moment that faith is born.

The gift of the Spirit is a promise to the disciples, but it is more than that. It is also an announcement that the lawsuit God began against the world in the earthly history of Jesus has now been decided, with the victory going to God and him whom he sent. It is Jesus' judges who are being judged. In the witness of the Spirit the condemned One becomes the judge (16:5 f.). Although this announcement of judgment still echoes the language of Jewish and early Christian apocalyptic, it contains nothing about a supranatural drama at the end. All we hear of is an event in history, an event which has its center in the death of Jesus upon the cross.

Like Paul and Mark, the Gospel of John has a "theology of the cross," albeit of a different kind. Its most radical expression occurs in the paradoxical assertion that Jesus' deepest humiliation coincided with his exaltation; the "hour" of his death was the hour of his "glorification" (3:12 ff.; 6:63 ff.; 12:23 ff., 32 f.; 13:1, 31 ff.; 17:1 ff.). John does not regard the death of Jesus as a passing episode in which a mythical divinity who came from heaven returns to the glory from which he came. It is rather a supremely real event, the triumph of the heavenly glory viewed and interpreted with the eyes of faith. What unbelief cannot see, being blind and lost in the world, is for faith a certainty. In the surrender of his Son God's saving love for the world became an event (3:16), reaching its climax in the service Jesus performed for his disciples (the foot-washing, 13:1 ff.). This event in turn becomes the foundation of the disciples' love for one another. Exemplified before their very eyes, this event of love is his bequest, the pledge of enduring fellowship with him (13:31 ff.; 15:1 ff.). Amid all their fear and despair they have the promise that the Lord will be victorious, not just in some later apocalyptic future, but already here and now (16:33).

It is obvious that John, like Mark, subjected his available traditions to critical evaluation in the light of his own theology of the cross. Take for instance his treatment of the passion. The cross casts its shadow from the outset of Jesus' ministry, and there are constantly recurring signals which point to the end. The first occurs in the testimony of the Baptist (1:26, 29), the next in the reference to Jesus' "hour" in the story of Cana. There is another in the cleansing of the Temple (2:13 ff.) which, for programmatic reasons, John places early in the ministry. And so it goes all through the Gospel. Hence, too, the sharp criticism of a faith based merely on miracles (4:48). John has no use for a Jesus who fulfills what the world expects of him, who uses his miraculous powers to his own advantage. For John there are no visible or tangible proofs which can serve as a ground for faith. But when faith is grounded in the word of the crucified Jesus, it can perceive his glory shining back upon the history of the earthly One.

John has reflected upon this revelation more profoundly than any other writer, and has articulated it with a one-sidedness which, though sometimes monotonous, is truly magnificent. Christianity today has every reason to rejoice that we have the synoptic Gospels as well as John. But it has no less reason to let John open up that dimension of faith which views the history of Jesus as a transaction between God and the world.

The First Letter of John shows that the Fourth Gospel had some influence, though at first it was confined to particular Johannine communities. (The Second Letter is ignored here since it has nothing new to contribute to Christian thought.) First John takes up a number of major themes adumbrated in the Gospel and applies them to the faith and life of the community in a series of meditations, themes such as the divine sonship of the believer and brotherly love, confession of sins and freedom from sin, faith and false doctrine.

In language and thought the letter is closely akin to the Gospel of John. But it has a narrower outlook, confined to the church. Traditional doctrines of early Christianity, relegated to the background in the Gospel, are emphasized once more. This is particularly true of the sacraments (5:5 ff.), the struggle with heresy (2:18 ff.; 4:1 ff.), and eschatology, which the letter relegates entirely to the future (2:1 ff.). This makes it unlikely that both works come from the same author. The tendency of First John is to assimilate Johannine thought to conventional Christianity, a tendency discernible at certain places in the Gospel which have been worked over and added to by a later hand. This tendency is especially evident in John 6:51–58 (the Lord's Supper, whose institution is not mentioned in John 13) and in John 5:27 ff. (the resurrection of the dead and the Last Judgment).

Conclusion:
The Common Theme
of the New Testament

The reader who has followed our treatment of the New Testament writings and pondered the questions we have considered may be astonished, perhaps even disturbed, by the diversity of early Christian faith and witness. He may shake his head in amazement at the variety of different interpretations of Jesus of Nazareth—especially if he has till now given the matter little thought and raised no questions concerning it. Can we still hear the voice of Jesus above the babel of other tongues? We hear it, of course, only through those who believed in him and who, within their own limitations and in the language of their own day, bore witness to their faith. That is why it is difficult to derive—in the case of either Testament—a uniform and timeless system of doctrine from the canonical writings. In neither Testament does God's revelation proceed in a smoothly flowing stream.

In this connection, however, it is the New Testament that has more to offer, because all of its books confront us with but a single theme. This common theme, which provides the clue to an understanding of the whole, is Jesus Christ and his history interpreted as a divine event of final and decisive significance. Thus the New Testament writings actually pass on Jesus' word insofar as they answer, each in its own way, to the question, not so much of who he *was,* but of who he *is.* They keep this question alive, ever open to a new response to God's challenge and to the salvation he offers the world in Christ.

We must break with our habit of all too easily regarding these various witnesses as distinct voices in one harmonious chorus, or—to use another popular image—the New Testament itself as a prism through which we can see the light of revelation refracted in all the colors of the rainbow. Such aesthetic comparisons falsify the situation rather than clarifying it. A careful reading will soon show that the New Testament, despite major agreements, is full of discords. Sometimes its numerous answers enshrine a genuine faith which preserves and applies anew the original word of Jesus. Sometimes they fall back on familiar traditions, producing interpretations of faith which tend to error, even to downright misinterpretation.

In this struggle of the spirits the Christian church continues to have a part. It must not be content with a merely passive role. It faces the same question as the outside world. Is this Jesus, who in human eyes met his end on the cross, a "scandal" as he was for the Jews in the time of Paul? Is he "nonsense" as he was for the Greeks? Or is the crucified One the power and wisdom of God (1 Cor. 1:18–25)? He is the same yesterday and today, and the people to whom the Christian message is addressed today are very much like the people it spoke to then.

Into the orbit of this event, decisive as it is for time and eternity, each succeeding generation is drawn by Jesus Christ himself. Thus the New Testament is the "charter" of Christian faith—and not just in the historian's sense of the word. The history of this faith will continue to be what it always was, the story of Jesus' passion—and the story of his resurrection.

Bibliography

Indexes

Bibliography

[Nontechnical works intelligible to the general reader are marked
*. Works from the author's original bibliography are included
here only if they are available in English translation. English
equivalents for his other listings have been selected by us and
are marked †.—Trans.]

DICTIONARIES

† Buttrick, George, ed. *The Interpreter's Dictionary of the Bible.*
4 vols. New York: Abingdon, 1962.

* Richardson, Alan, ed. *A Word Book of the New Testament.*
London: SCM, 1950.

HISTORY OF NEW TESTAMENT CRITICISM

†* Fuller, Reginald H. *The New Testament in Current Study.*
New York: Scribner's, 1962.

Kümmel, Werner. *The New Testament: The History of the Investigation of Its Problems.* Translated by S. MacLean Gilmour
and Howard C. Kee. Nashville: Abingdon, 1972.

†* Neill, Stephen. *The Interpretation of the New Testament.*
London and New York: Oxford University, 1964.

†* Via, Dan O., ed. Guides to Biblical Scholarship—New Testament Series. Philadelphia: Fortress, 1969–.

EDITIONS OF THE TEXT

a. Greek

Huck, Albert; Lietzmann, Hans; and Cross, F. L. *Synopsis of the First Three Gospels*. 9th ed. Tübingen: J. C. B. Mohr, 1936.

Nestle, E., and Aland, Kurt, eds. *Novum testamentum graece*. 25th ed. Stuttgart: Würtembergische Bibelanstalt, 1963.

b. In English Translation

†* *The Holy Bible: Revised Standard Version*. New York: Nelson, 1952. [This is the most literal of the modern translations.]

†* *The New English Bible with the Apocrypha*. Oxford University and Cambridge University, 1970.

†* Jones, Alexander, ed. *The Jerusalem Bible*. Garden City, N.Y.: Doubleday, 1966.

†* *Gospel Parallels: A Synopsis of the First Three Gospels*. New York: Nelson, 1949.

c. Apocrypha of the New Testament

Hennecke, Edgar. *New Testament Apocrypha*. Revised by W. Schneemelcher. Translated by R. McL. Wilson. 2 vols. Philadelphia: Westminster, 1963–65.

NEW TESTAMENT INTRODUCTION

Feine, P., and Behm, J. *Introduction to the New Testament*. Revised by Werner Kümmel. Translated by A. J. Matill, Jr. New York and Nashville: Abingdon, 1965.

†* Fuller, Reginald H. *A Critical Introduction to the New Testament*. Naperville, Ill.: Allenson, 1966.

* Marxsen, Willi. *Introduction to the New Testament*. Translated by G. Buswell. Philadelphia: Fortress, 1968.

THEOLOGY OF THE NEW TESTAMENT

Bultmann, Rudolf. *Theology of the New Testament*. Translated by K. Grobel. 2 vols. New York: Scribner's, 1951–55.

Conzelmann, Hans. *An Outline of New Testament Theology*. Translated by J. Bowden. New York: Harper & Row, 1969.

ENVIRONMENT AND HISTORY
OF EARLIEST CHRISTIANITY

* Bultmann, Rudolf. *Primitive Christianity in Its Contemporary Setting.* Translated by Reginald H. Fuller. New York: Thames & Hudson, 1956.

Reicke, Bo. *The New Testament Era.* Translated by David E. Green. Philadelphia: Fortress, 1968.

†* Schultz, H. J. *Jesus in His Time.* Philadelphia: Fortress, 1971.

COMMENTARIES AND SERIES

† Albright, William F., and Freedman, David N., eds. The Anchor Bible. Garden City, N.Y.: Doubleday, 1964–.

†* Ackroyd, P. R.; Leaney, A. R. C.; and Packer, J. W., eds. The Cambridge Bible Commentary: New English Bible. Cambridge: At the University, 1963–.

† Hermeneia: A Critical and Historical Commentary on the Bible. Philadelphia: Fortress, 1971–.

†*Nineham, Dennis E., ed. The Pelican Gospel Commentaries. Baltimore and Harmonsworth, England: Penguin, 1963–68.

Wickenhauser, Alfred, and Kuss, Otto, eds. Regensburg New Testament Commentary. Staten Island, N.Y.: Alba, 1968–.

CANON

† Grant, Robert M. *The Formation of the New Testament.* New York: Harper & Row, 1965.

1. JESUS AND THE GOSPEL

a. The Message of Jesus

Bornkamm, Günther. *Jesus of Nazareth.* Translated by I. and F. McCluskey with J. M. Robinson. New York: Harper & Row, 1961.

Bultmann, Rudolf. *Jesus and the Word.* Translated by L. P. Smith and E. H. Lantero. New York: Scribner's, 1934; paperback ed., 1958.

Jeremias, Joachim. *New Testament Theology: The Proclamation of Jesus.* Vol. 1. Translated by J. Bowden. New York: Scribner's, 1971. [The American edition of the English translation nowhere indicates that this is volume 1.—Trans.]

Schweizer, E. *Jesus.* Translated by David E. Green. Richmond, Va.: John Knox, 1971. [The English title of this work is seriously misleading. The German title in English translation is: "Jesus Christ in the manifold testimony of the New Testament."—Trans.]

b. *The Gospel and the Gospels*

Braaten, C. E., and Harrisville, R.A., eds. and trans. *The Historical Jesus and the Kerygmatic Christ.* Nashville and New York: Abingdon, 1962. [This book bears the same title as the German volume listed by Bornkamm, but the essays represent an entirely different selection from the debate on the new quest of the historical Jesus, with two exceptions, the essays by Ethelbert Stauffer and Rudolf Bultmann. Bultmann's essay, translated in full in the Braaten-Harrisville volume, was given only in précis in the German volume. The following essays from the German volume are also available in English:

> Cullmann, Oscar. "Out of Season Remarks on the Historical Jesus of the Bultmann School." *Union Seminary Quarterly Review* 16 (1961): 131–48.
>
> Fuchs, E. "Jesus' Understanding of Time." In *Studies of the Historical Jesus,* pp. 104–66. Naperville, Ill.: Allenson, 1964 (an expansion of the essay in the German volume).
>
> Käsemann, Ernst. "The Problem of the Historical Jesus." In *Essays on New Testament Themes,* by Ernst Käsemann, pp. 15–47. Naperville, Ill.: Allenson, 1964 (the essay which according to James M. Robinson inaugurated the new quest).
>
> Reicke, Bo. "Incarnation and Exaltation." *Interpretation* 16 (1962): 156–68.—Trans.]

Robinson, James M. *A New Quest of the Historical Jesus.* Naperville, Ill.: Allenson, 1959. [The German edition cited by the author is later than the English, and contains additional material which has not been included in later editions of the English version.—Trans.]

2. THE SYNOPTIC GOSPELS

a. The Sources

†* Bea, Augustin. *The Study of the Synoptic Gospels.* New York: Harper & Row, 1965.

b. The Earliest Jesus Tradition

Bultmann, Rudolf. *The History of the Synoptic Tradition.* 2nd ed. Translated by John Marsh. Oxford: Blackwell, 1968. [It is important to read the revised translation, as the first English edition (1963) was poorly translated and is often misleading. —Trans.]

Bultmann, Rudolf. "The Study of the Synoptic Gospels." In *Form Criticism: A New Method of New Testament Research,* edited and translated by F. C. Grant. Chicago and New York: Willet, Clark, 1934.

Dibelius, Martin. *From Tradition to Gospel.* Translated by B. L. Woolf. New York: Scribner's, 1935.

† Perrin, Norman. *Rediscovering the Teaching of Jesus.* New York and Evanston: Harper & Row, 1967.

c. Types of the Christ-Message

†* Fuller, Reginald H. *The Formation of the Resurrection Narratives.* New York: Macmillan, 1971.

Lohse, Eduard. *History of the Suffering and Death of Jesus Christ.* Translated by M. O. Dietrich. Philadelphia: Fortress, 1967.

†* Marxsen, Willi. *The Resurrection of Jesus of Nazareth.* Translated by Margaret Kohl. Philadelphia: Fortress, 1970.

Robinson, James M., and Koester, Helmut. *Trajectories through Early Christianity.* Philadelphia: Fortress, 1967.

d. Matthew—Mark—Luke

1. Mark

Marxsen, Willi. *Mark the Evangelist.* Translated by J. Boyce et al. with R. A. Harrisville. Nashville and New York: Abingdon, 1969.

†Weeden, Theodore J. *Mark—Traditions in Conflict.* Philadelphia: Fortress, 1971.

2. Matthew

Bornkamm, Günther; Barth, G.; and Held, H. J. *Tradition and Interpretation in Matthew*. Philadelphia: Westminster, 1963.

3. Luke

Conzelmann, Hans. *The Theology of St. Luke*. New York: Harper & Row, 1960. [The original German *Die Mitte der Zeit* was revised a number of times, the revision of 1964—which Bornkamm lists—being the last revision. The English translation was based on the edition of 1957.—Trans.]

3. THE GOSPEL ACCORDING TO PAUL

* Bornkamm, Günther. *Paul*. Translated by D. M. G. Stalker. New York and Evanston: Harper & Row, 1969.
* Dibelius, Martin. *Paul*. Edited by Werner Kümmel. Translated by F. Clarke. Philadelphia: Westminster, 1953.

Käsemann, Ernst. *Perspectives on Paul*. Translated by Margaret Kohl. Philadelphia: Fortress, 1969.

4. THE LATER WRITINGS OF THE
NEW TESTAMENT: THE FOURTH GOSPEL

Bornkamm, Günther. *Early Christian Experience*. Translated by P. L. Hammer. New York: Harper & Row, 1969. [This is an English translation of selected essays from the first two of the four volumes of collected essays listed by Bornkamm.—Trans.]

Brown, Raymond, ed. and trans. *The Gospel According to John*. 2 vols. The Anchor Bible. Garden City, N.Y.: Doubleday, 1966–70.

Bultmann, Rudolf. *The Gospel of John*. Edited and translated by G. R. Beasley-Murray et al. Philadelphia: Westminster, 1971.

Käsemann, Ernst. *The Testament of Jesus*. Translated by G. Krodel. Philadelphia: Fortress, 1966.

Schnackenburg, Rudolf. *The Gospel According to St. John*. Vol. 1. Translated by K. Smith. New York: Herder & Herder, 1963.

Indexes

NAMES

SUBJECTS

SCRIPTURE REFERENCES

OLD TESTAMENT

Genesis
1:31 — 45 f.

Psalms
110 — 125

Isaiah
35:5 f. — 46

Jeremiah
31:31 — 5
38:31 — 5

NEW TESTAMENT

Matthew
1 — 34
4 — 34
4:1–11 — 59
4:4 ff. — 42
4:15 f. — 62
4:17 — 15, 65
5–7 — 27
5:1 — 34
5:3 ff. — 14, 62
5:17 — 60
5:17 ff. — 59
5:17–19 — 59
5:18 f. — 59
5:20 — 59
5:21–48 — 60
6 — 14
6:9 ff. — 27
6:25 ff. — 35
7:15 ff. — 119
7:21 ff. — 59
7:22 — 59
7:24 — 62
7:29 — 60
8:5 ff. — 26, 42
8:17 — 62
9:9 — 58
9:36 — 62
10 — 60

10:3 — 58
11:2–6 — 38
11:5 — 46
12:18 ff. — 62
12:25 ff. — 42
12:38 ff. — 42
12:41–42 — 42
12:43 ff. — 42
13 — 27, 60
13:14 ff. — 28
13:16 f. — 13
13:24 ff. — 13
13:31 f. — 13
13:33 f. — 13
13:36 ff. — 28, 62
13:44 ff. — 13
13:47 ff. — 28, 62
13:52 — 41
13:55 — 34
14:28 ff. — 28
15:28 — 46
16:16 ff. — 28
16:18 — 61
17:22 ff. — 66
18 — 61
18:23 ff. — 13, 28
20:1 ff. — 13, 28
21:25 ff. — 66
21:28 — 28
22:14 — 62
23 — 60
23:8 — 60
24–25 — 60
25:31 ff. — 28, 62
26 — 34
26–27 — 47
26:29 — 48
27 — 46, 49
28 — 34
28:19 — 61
28:20 — 62

Mark
1–8 — 52, 53
1:1 — 51

1:1–15 — 53
1:11 — 55
1:12 f. — 54
1:15 — 10, 65
1:16–20 — 53
1:21–28 — 53
1:24 — 45
1:27 — 53
1:32 ff. — 45
1:34 — 55
1:44 — 55
2:1–12 — 53
2:6–10 — 53
2:10 — 55
2:13 ff. — 54
2:19 f. — 57
2:22 — 54
2:28 — 55
3:1–5 — 53
3:6 — 57
3:7 ff. — 45
3:11 — 45
3:12 — 55
3:27 — 13, 45
4 — 43
4:10–12 — 55
4:26 ff. — 28
4:35–5:43 — 46
5:1–19 — 45
5:7 — 46
5:28 ff. — 45
5:34 — 46
5:41 — 36
5:43 — 55
6:3 — 34
6:53 ff. — 45
7:26 — 55
7:31–37 — 45
7:32 ff. — 28
7:34 — 36
8:22 ff. — 28
8:26 — 53
8:27–10:52 — 57
8:30 — 55
8:31 — 48, 55